Sister Odell has truly turned her pain into purpose. This is a story of hope arising from grief. It underscores the critical need for us as Black people to create a culture of emotional emancipation, healing, wellness, and empowerment in every community in which we live.

ENOLA G. AIRD, FOUNDER AND PRESIDENT,
COMMUNITY HEALING NETWORK, INC.

TESTIMONIALS

We as human beings are storytellers. We create and tell stories to give meaning to our experiences. The stories we share shape our lives and our relationship with other people. No matter how painful, complex, beautiful, or simple a story can liberate and heal us. The Rev. Odell Cooper's "Interruptions" takes us on a journey of pain and promise. Most importantly, it is a story that opens a window for our soul and mind to the healing power of hope.

REV. DR. FREDERICK (JERRY) STREETS

"Interruptions" is a story all too commonly shared within urban communities, a tragedy repeated in an endless cycle of unnecessary violence until a brave few stand up to disrupt the cycle and repair the shared trauma it leaves behind. Rev. Odell Montgomery Cooper's first-hand account of the trauma she experienced as she details the devastating event of losing her son to gun violence, her resilience, and her awe-inspiring journey towards ensuring the cycle of violence is broken within urban communities make a lasting difference that reverberates throughout her book. Her story needs to be heard, shared, and understood so that our communities may follow the same journey of healing she has gone through to end this needless violence.

MAYSA AKBAR

Regardless of a person's gender, ethnicity, race, or economic status, life without surprises does not exist. We can be ever so prepared and yet experience an unexpected turn in life's journey that leaves us depleted and lifeless. The book "Interruptions" was written to jump-start the person left for dead because of trauma, violence, and heartache. Allow the pages of this riveting book to produce the healing process needed to deal with life's future interruptions.

JONATHAN J. SHEPHERD, M.D.

The unpredictability of life places mind-blowing challenges upon everyone. This is the nature of the human experience. The reality of how we respond to the interruptions of our planned journey is the defining factor of true character. This book is a testament to resilience in the battle for equanimity throughout the ups and downs of life.

BISHOP BENJAMIN K. WATTS, BLACK MINISTRIES PROGRAM, DIRECTOR, HARTFORD SEMINARY

Reverend Odell Montgomery Cooper has written a powerful story that clearly demonstrates the indwelling presence of the Holy Spirit in her life. She used that which was meant for evil and made it something that glorified God, Genesis 50:20. Her personal testimony is a witness of what it means to surrender all to God and allow ourselves to be used as an instrument of faith, hope, and love. So, people will see and know that God still reigns. Taste and see!!!

JAY MORRIS, PH.D., JD, MA, PCC VICE PRESIDENT,
LEARNING AND DEVELOPMENT YALE-NEW HAVEN HEALTH SYSTEM

Odell is an example of the importance of prioritizing mental health in the face of trauma, loss, and all the ways life and society can undermine one's well-being and sense of self. When life assaults and destroys peace and sanity, life also offers opportunities for reclaiming them through restorative practices up to and including mental health counseling. Learning how she was able to rise from devastation and stand for the healing of victims of violence and despair is an inspirational lesson.

DAVID ADDAMS

When you are going through rough times, it can be very hard to make the connection to your wellness. But taking control of your wellness can be the necessary breakthrough that you need towards wholeness. Your mind, body, and spirit are all connected. It is critically important to your long-term success that you find a way to succeed in all of these areas. Odell's story is a true testament towards this journey, and it is hard, but it is possible.

DR. CHAKA FELDER-MCENTIRE (CERTIFIED PERSONAL FITNESS TRAINER)

Join me in breaking
the chains of
generational
trauma

Rev. O

11/21

DISRUPTING THE SILENCE

REV. ODELL MONTGOMERY COOPER

JEWELL JORDAN PUBLISHING LLC
OKLAHOMA

For information, address Jewell Jordan Publishing, LLC 1205 South Air Depot Blvd, Suite 153, Midwest City, Oklahoma 73110

Cover Design and Book Illustrations by Anna Bovi
Interior Design by The Roberts Group
Interior Photographs courtesy of the Author

Library of Congress Control Number: 2021919049

Paperback ISBN: 978-1-7360906-4-0
eBook ISBN: 978-1-7360906-5-7

First Edition

Printed in the United States of America

DEDICATION

In loving memory of my son
Jonathan Michael Cooper (Coop)
Nov 15, 1990–Apr. 23, 2016

Daughter Jackie

our next generations:
Duke III, Malika, Kyle, Nicholas, Maya, Peyton,
Danny and Damar, Jr.

CONTENTS

SPECIAL ACKNOWLEDGEMENTS

Dr. Edward Rippel, Dr. Hadar Lubin, Anne Watkins, Jonathan Q. Berryman, Mrs. Betty Hill, Thompson elders, Margarette Gulinello, Dominique Pascascio, Melissa Lamy, Morgan Rollins, David Adams, Jay Morris, Michelle Turner, KimBianca Williams, Rob Archibald, Cathy Patton, IDS Leadership Team, Nichelle Davis, Tanya Morgan, Darsweil Rogers, all those who prayed without ceasing when the doctors said stop and the distinguished Divine 9. Much love to my nephew, Norris Morgan, Jr., for encouraging me to share my truth.

FOREWORD

SOMETHING COMPELLED ME TO ASK. I couldn't escape the unction. I thought that my point in going to this political fundraiser was to meet, greet, and eat, but the Spirit of the Living God had an additional plan—reconnecting with Odell Montgomery Cooper and inspiring her ministry.

While meeting, greeting, and eating, I was able to catch up with Odell, who I had not seen in some time. When I asked her what she was doing, she told me she was reinventing herself. That statement stuck with me even as I went on to converse with other guests at the cookout. During those other conversations, I repeatedly heard, "Go back and ask her." Little did I know that being obedient to the Spirit would plant a seed from which a ministry of healing would blossom.

"Odell, what do you mean you're reinventing yourself?" Odell began to tell her story. The Spirit spoke to me again. "Tell her, *you should tell your story through the arts. It will help people heal.*" Odell immediately proclaimed that she was not an artist, but as God had done for the prophets of the past, provision for her work had already been made.

Thank you, Odell, for hearing God's voice and heeding the call to become a "Moses" to the grieved—building the community's capacity to tell Trauma, "LET MY PEOPLE GO!"

Jonathan Q. Berryman

MESSAGE FROM THE AUTHOR

THERE WAS A TIME WHEN I had different dreams. I followed my mother's advice by sitting up straight, never living with a man, finishing college, getting a good job, getting married, and having kids. My Nana introduced me to God and encouraged me to stay connected, while my Aunt Eleanor said never to leave work and go straight home. My brother said, "You are a Montgomery! You have what it takes to excel academically; you are a survivor." As a young girl, I believed I would be happy and successful if I followed all this advice. But their advice never prepared me for the *Interruption*. No one in my family prepared me for the day I lost my son to gun violence in a case of mistaken identity, making April 23rd at 2:00 a.m. more than the worst day of my life!

I believed that my residential zip code, education, lifestyle, and family values were enough to protect my family from frequent gun violence in and toward communities of color.

As an ordained minister, I was accustomed to providing comfort and support to families during their time of grief. The healing scriptures would roll off my tongue, and cliche healing statements often followed. The phrases "keep the faith," "God is with you," "keep praying" were words I believed would comfort their pain—until it happened to me.

Some things my family, culture, and faith taught me about grief were useless. No one ever mentioned the words "Traumatic Grief." Between the reality of his death, deceit, and the painful police investigation, I suffered a brain aneurysm on John's birthdate. All the advice from my family and culture about being a strong Black woman, I had to dismiss and learn that I am a Black woman who is strong and sometimes weak. In the moments of being weak, I learned to ask for help in order to survive.

I rediscovered God in a way that was refreshing and healing. At my lowest and darkest period in life, I fought to live. I fought to break the cycle of generational trauma. I fought not to destroy the remaining years of my daughter's life by dying on her brother's birthdate. Jonathan was born to keep her company; he was the light, the bridge between our mother-daughter relationship. We both needed him to be present in our lives. And when our light was gone, we both felt the darkness.

When the spirit of Jesus began hovering over my body lying in a hospital bed after surgery, it was then that I gave God the pain I was carrying so I could fight for my life. If Jesus needed to take something back to God, take this pain because I wanted to live. God accepted the compromise but left me with many health and life challenges. These challenges changed everything in my daily lifestyle. Being stubborn, I pushed back and tried to reclaim the lifestyle I was accustomed to before the surgery and failed miserably every time, year after year. Today, I have finally surrendered to the will of God, and I am learning to accept that I am living God's dream for my life, not my own.

Thank you for reading and talking about my book Interruptions, and I ask that you join me in disrupting the silence of pain and trauma that our culture encourages us to keep silent. The frequent occurrence of gun violence in and toward communities of color lead to similar layers of stressors in an already strained environment. Nonetheless, Interruptions intends to 'Disrupt the Silence' on these traumas and begin to break the stigmas to mental health and create a path of healing.

I hope you are motivated and willing to share this book with others and join me in breaking generational trauma to reunite with your faith and believe that you, too, can be happy with the will of God for your life.

Rev. O

CHAPTER 1
FIRST INTERRUPTION: IT'S A GIRL

I OFTEN WONDERED WHETHER MY BIRTH was a mistake, or did my mother have a change of heart and ask God for a child? Either way, I was born to aging parents, and my birth was an interruption to their lives. My mother was born as an only child, raised and educated in private schools in Beverly, Massachusetts, while her mother, Odell Haywood, was a widow, who worked and lived in a one-bedroom servant quarters caring for a rich White family in Chestnut Hill, Massachusetts, a rich White suburban community with mansions and family estates.

After my mother graduated high school, she perfected her culinary skills and moved to New York City, where she also began working for rich families on the East Side of Manhattan, but as their private chef. Our family research shows that my father, Benjamin Duke Montgomery, who everyone called Duke, was one of 11 children born to parents in Savannah, Georgia. His parents were once slaves and then sharecroppers. At some point during his childhood the siblings were separated and sent to live with various relatives who raised them. My father was charismatic, handsome at 6-feet tall, thick-framed and always well-dressed, with velvety, dark chocolate skin and a deep voice, smooth as Barry White's. When he walked into a room, his presence demanded attention. I learned my father was partially illiterate but it was unnoticeable. Duke enlisted in the Army at the age of 16, married and never divorced at least four women, fathered children and later claimed Harlem as his home. No one in the family has been able to share the details of how my mother, an educated woman, met and fell in love with my father, but I was told, he swept my mother off her feet. Growing up, they never shared stories of how they met. All I knew was that my mother never wanted children and I was a surprise to the entire family. I heard family members could not believe that a 40-year-old woman was pregnant. Some people thought she had a tumor instead. When I was born, my mother was a successful chef and my father was 51 years old and worked as a skycap for Trans World Airlines (TWA) earning great tips from travelers. I remember as a child pretending to be sleep on the couch watching him come home and pulling rolls of dollar bills out of every pocket and then handing the money over to my mother.

When I was born, my parents, Duke and Mary Montgomery, lived in a one-bedroom apartment overlooking the busy city streets of Harlem, on 116th Street and 7th Avenue. Their apartment was not filled with a baby crib, a decorated room for a baby girl, new toys, or diapers for a newborn. Other than seeing a pregnant woman climb the stairs to reach their second-floor apartment, there were no signs of a baby coming soon. I wondered what gossip the neighbors had about this old woman having a baby and never seeing the couple bringing home baby clothes and then one day, no baby!

Several family members tell this story differently, but either way, three days after my birth, I was wrapped in a blanket leaving Harlem Hospital coddled for the next three hours in a car headed to Boston, Massachusetts. Later in life, I saw pictures of me sleeping in a laundry basket, wearing a diaper and a T-shirt. They caused me to reflect on my birth and the lives that were interrupted on March 9, 1962.

My parents named me Odell Leila Montgomery, Odell after my maternal grandmother and Leila after my paternal grandmother. My paternal grandmother died before I was born. I called my maternal grandmother Nana. After I was born, Nana arranged for me to live with her niece, Doretha, whom I would call "Momma Doe." My family had to develop a unique way of identifying me because there were three of us in the family named Odell. My Nana was called "Auntie Odell," my cousin was called "Big Dell," and I was called "Little Odell."

Momma Doe's three children are my biological cousins, but I called them my sisters and brothers. Momma Doe's son, Thomas, the oldest, was grown and lived on the road driving interstate tractor-trailers; he was tall and always wore cowboy boots, big brim hats and shiny belt buckles. JoAnn, the middle child, had long red hair. She was a teenager and I mostly remember her sitting on the couch hugging a pillow, playing the 45-record over and over while singing "Please Mr. Postman, is there a letter in your bag for me. It's been a very long time since I heard from this boyfriend of mine, there must be some word today" by the Marvelettes. Charlene was Momma Doe's youngest daughter and was six years older than me. By the time I started first grade, JoAnn had obviously received her letter, left Boston and married her boyfriend Roger once he was discharged from the Marines. They moved to his hometown, Farmville, North Carolina, and had two boys. Now Charlene was the oldest in the house and I was the baby sister. Charlene used to sit me on her lap like I was her baby doll.

My Nana had two days off a week, Sunday and Thursday. On those days, Momma Doe would would pick Nana up in the morning and drive her to our home for dinner, returning her to Chestnut Hills after dinner. On Sundays, Nana took me to church at Grant AME on Washington Street. On Thursdays, she would bring me one roll of multi-flavored Life Savers, which I never wanted to share with Charlene because it was from my Nana. I never asked why she only had one roll and I did not really care. It was the one day of the week where I was made to feel special and I loved it.

My Nana loved the Boston Red Sox baseball team and listened to each game on her small transistor radio that she carried with her. She also loved playing poker—mostly during family gatherings—and spoiling me. Nana was 64 years old when I was born and always old to me. She carried a red pocketbook and wore a corset with red dresses and a white monogrammed handkerchief tucked into the side of the belt. Her gray wig had an artificial red rose tucked in the side near her right ear. My Nana had a distinctive laugh that was contagious and jolly. When she laughed, everyone in the room would smile and laugh, too. She was the fifth of 12 Thompson children. All my great aunts and uncles lived in Boston except for the oldest sister, Minnie Rogers, who remained in their hometown, Bradenton, Florida. My Great-Aunt Minnie and her husband had a huge family and were the first Black licensed undertakers in the state. I had the pleasure of spending spring breaks or long weekends with a host of family members and many cousins in Boston and Bradenton, Florida.

Nana and her siblings were close. They lived next door or within 5-minute drives to one another in Boson. We always spent holidays together. They enjoyed playing poker whenever they could, which became a staple signature of the Thompson family in Boston. The moment the kitchen was cleaned from dinner, the cards came out, along with rolls of quarters and dollar bills. It was time to play poker. Who was winning determined what time we left the house.

During the week at Momma Doe's, we had a routine: school, homework, playtime, and dinner was always ready at 6 p.m. I had to set the dinner table while Charlene was learning how to cook. I was too short to reach the dishes, so Charlene found a stool for me to stand on to dry the dishes. Afterward, Momma Doe would mop the kitchen floor, turn off the lights and no one dared to enter for any reason. Momma Doe's house was always spotless. Every Saturday morning, we cleaned the house. My job was to dust every nick knack and table leg, and Charlene vacuumed.

Growing up, I either played in my bedroom or outside in the neighborhood, as long as I was home by the time the streets lights came on. One day before dinner Momma Doe gave me an envelope and told me to walk to the corner and place it in the mailbox. As I walked to the mailbox, a neighbor boy from my first grade class who I had a crush on walked up to me and we started talking. I walked right by the mailbox and into the corner store with him. Inside playing, he chased me around the store as I laughed and giggled. The next thing I knew the envelope fell out of my hand, sliding underneath a cabinet. I bent down and couldn't reach the envelope, so I got scared and ran out of the store. At home, Momma Doe asked whether I mailed her letter. I looked at her with a straight face, and without stuttering, said yes. She told me to get ready for dinner. Two minutes later I heard a knock at the door. It was the owner of the store.

"Your daughter was in the store, and I noticed that she dropped your envelope, so I wanted to make sure that you received it because it looked like it was a bill," I heard him saying.

Momma Doe looked at him, said "thank you" and shut the door. The next thing I heard was "Dell come here!" Momma Doe showed me the envelope.

"You lied to me," she said. "You told me that you mailed my insurance bill. This is my money order to pay for my car insurance."

Something seemed to grow out of her right arm and came swinging in my direction, meeting my bare legs. It was Momma Does' belt. With each lash, I heard, "You lied to me, stop crying. You said you mailed it, stop crying. I always pay my bills on time, stop crying. I'm never late with my bills, stop crying." After what seemed like an eternity, but was only minutes later, I was able to get up off the floor and go to my room. Charlene was in the corner looking at me. When we finished dinner, I took a bath and went to bed. I thought about Charlene and said to myself, "I am going to get her, she didn't help me."

One Christmas, I received a tiny porcelain China tea set with cups that only held a few drops of water. On rainy days I would host tea parties in our bedroom. Charlene and I shared the same bedroom, which contained two twin beds pushed against the walls. We each had our own 4-drawer dresser, a nightstand and a small multi-colored, knitted rug in the center of the floor. I would invite Charlene and our cousin Sarah, who lived next door, to the tea parties. Sarah's mother and Nana were sisters. Sarah was chubby with long, thick hair, and she wore cat eyeglasses.

Charlene, being the oldest, was often responsible for watching us. We were always together. Growing up, I had a speech impediment, and I always stuttered. As a result, family members either completed my sentences, would hit me on my back to make me spit the words out of my mouth, or avoided asking me questions that required a lengthy response. I was the only one in the family with a speech impediment and was teased mercilessly. Charlene always made me leave the room to refill the small teapot with fresh water. Instead of getting water from the sink, which I could not reach, I refilled the pot from the toilet.

When I returned, she and Sarah had eaten all the cookies and I began to cry. Momma Doe ran into the room to make sure everything was alright. By the time I could get the words out of my mouth, Charlene would tell a different story and Momma Doe believed her. Sarah did not care because she had already eaten the cookies. But little did she know this was the beginning of Charlene bossing both of us around. When Momma Doe left the room, Charlene looked at us and said, "Stop crying or I'm going to get you." We didn't know what that meant but she was taller, and the words seemed scary, so we did what she told us. This didn't stop me from hosting tea parties and using the toilet water to refill the pot. These parties always ended the same way, except Momma Doe stopped running in the room and would instead yell "CUT IT OUT," and we did.

YEARS LATER

Being teased as a stutterer was tortuous. My family would say, "You can tell when Dell is lying because she stutters." Shoot, I stuttered even when I wasn't lying but lying intensified the stammering. One day, I will enjoy telling Sarah and Charlene that they were drinking toilet water with my cookies. If they read this book then the secret is out the bag.

I was about ten years old when Momma Doe purchased a new stereo console. It looked like a wooden dining cabinet, and the entire lid lifted up and revealed the record player and knobs to adjust the volume and bass. In the corner of the player you could store 45 rpm records and the yellow disc adapter placed in the hole in the middle of a record before loading it on the player. The stereo console was about 6-feet long and sat in the living room, a room never entered without permission. With music playing, the tea set was put away to make room while Charlene taught us the new dances. Charlene and Sarah pretended to be either the Jackson 5 or Diana Ross and the Supremes. They would stand in the open space between our beds in the middle of the room, singing and practicing new dance steps. Because I stuttered, they would not allow me to join their group. My assignment was to turn up the music or change the records for the next routine. Every weekend I asked to join the group, and Charlene replied, "No, you can't sing because you stutter." I dreaded just sitting on my bed or changing the records while watching the Sarah and Charlene show. Trying to intervene on my behalf, Momma Doe came into the room one day and asked Sarah and Charlene, "If she could find a song to sing, would you let her sing in the group?"

Charlene chuckled and said, "Sure." It was clear she did not believe that was possible.

Then one day turned out to be different. As usual, I came home from school planning to go into the bedroom to change my clothes before the singing duo began their performance with me as their lone audience member. As I walked into the apartment carrying my school bag, Momma Doe said, "I put something on the bed for you." It was a 45-record. Picking it up, I read the label and the name of the artist. Neither sounded familiar or even interesting.

"Who is this man?" I wondered, and "What is this song?" When I asked permission to play the record on the stereo, Momma Doe approved and smiled.

I walked into the living room, opened the lid on the stereo and placed the plastic disc in the center of the record. I turned on the stereo and put the needle on the record as it spun on the turntable and the music played. I sat next to the stereo so I could hear the song. It started with a drum solo and did not have much of a dance beat. However, something compelled me to listen to the entire song. Then it happened; magic echoed from the speakers. The artist was named Elton John, and the song was called "Benny and the Jets." All I could hear was him singing "B-B-B-B-B Benny and the Jets." I was so excited, I picked up the needle arm of the record player and played it again, and again, and again. Who was Elton John, and what were Benny and the Jets? I listened to this song for two hours. Unable to sing the words, I knew the hook, "B-B-B-B-B Benny and the Jets."

I was smiling; this night promised to be different with the new record. No more sitting on the bed watching them perform. You should have seen their faces when I played the record. I reminded them what they promised Momma Doe. Nonetheless, Charlene made me stand in the corner because I had only a small part. To this day, Sarah is the only Black person I know who can sing the correct lyrics to "Benny and the Jets." To this day, when the song plays on the radio, the three of us laugh, and Sarah still points to me so that I can sing the hook.

The recording changed my life—becoming my theme song, my mantra. It didn't stop me from stuttering, but singing the hook was wonderful. The song gave me goose bumps and I would sing the hook and giggle. I began looking for more songs like this. It felt as if Elton John knew me and I was not alone. What magic!

TWO MOTHERS

My first memory of my mother and realizing that I technically had two mothers and two different homes was around first grade. On the first day of school my mother came to Boston and walked me to school, came inside and met my teacher. They spoke in the corner then she left. But when the bell rang ending school, my mother was waiting outside. She held my hand and asked about my day. I just loved her soft hands and pleasant voice.

My parents still lived in Manhattan, but only my mother came to Boston on weekends, holidays, and always to celebrate my birthday. We had a party, including a cake or some special event. She made it a point to make me feel special and loved on my birthday. My cousins came to my birthday party looking forward to my mother's famous "Candy Land Money Cake." It was a three-layered vanilla cake with homemade frosting, topped with lollipops, gumdrops and bubble gum of all shapes and colors. Before she frosted the cake, my mother made me leave the kitchen. I would sneak around the corner and watch her wrap coins in foil—nickels and dimes—and place them around the cake before it was frosted. After singing the happy birthday song, my mother would cut the cake and hand out the slices. Everyone received a nickel or dime in their slice except me. My slice of cake always had the quarter. We all ate the cake and showed off our money. At the age of six, this was miraculous; the kids wondered how my mother did this trick every year. I didn't care; I had a quarter.

If my mother didn't come to Boston, Nana and I took the Greyhound bus to New York, and my mother picked us up at the Port Authority Bus Terminal. My mother wore practical, fashionable dresses and comfortable shoes. Carrying a brown designer tote bag and a pocketbook, she always looked as if she just got off work. Like most of the women in my family, she wore a wig; however, my mother did not wear makeup. Her skin was always smooth and glowing, and her hands were soft. My mother nicknamed me "Pumpkin." So, when I got off the bus, she touched my face with her soft hands and said, "Hi, Pumpkin!" Her voice was gentle and pleasant. Then we rode in a Yellow Cab to a restaurant on the East Side.

When we visited my parents in their one-bedroom apartment, Nana and I slept on the pull-out couch in the living room. Our home was exquisitely decorated. As you walked into the apartment, to the left was my father's walk-in closet. He had the only key and kept his eclectic album collection—Duke Ellington, Louis Armstrong, Bessie Smith, Hines, Hines and Dad, and others—locked in that closet. On the inside of the door was an oil painting of a naked Brazilian woman. I wondered: Who was this woman who posed for this painting, why did my father have this painting of her hanging on the closet door, and why did my mother refer to it as art?

The living room had a full bar with two swivel bar stools and a wall-mounted shelf with wine and shot glasses. I never understood the bar because my parents did not drink. Their one-bedroom apartment was tastefully decorated like one of those places in the Architectural Digest magazine. In the dining room was a wooden cabinet with my baby picture, a gold clock and a 5x7-inch picture of a semi-naked White woman who autographed her photo "to Duke." I guess this was art too!

The bedroom where my parents slept was off the hallway. The only big chair in their bedroom was my father's black leather recliner with a foot massager. The apartment smelled like fresh spring flowers. The artwork on the walls varied. There was framed artwork throughout the house except for the bathroom. Next to the shower was a velvet glow-in-the-dark poster with zodiac signs and sexual positions for each month. I enjoyed turning off the lights and watching it glow. It was obvious my parents had different tastes in art. I didn't understand it but was told it was art.

My visits were always magical excursions. My mother enjoyed the museums, Broadway musicals, dining at five-star restaurants, and clothes shopping at Macy's department store or in the garment district. During my special trips to the garment district with my mother, she often favored the vendors with boxes of her famous homemade, deep chocolate brownies with crushed walnuts. Once a vendor opened a package, the other staffers would smell the brownies and come running. While the vendors ate brownies, my mother and I enjoyed shopping, selecting anything we wanted from their fashion lines. These were not knock-offs but designer originals.

One summer Sarah joined my mother, Nana, and me on a trip to Mexico. Later, Charlene joined us on an excursion to Barbados. Soon the family began having the Rogers-Thompson-Dabney Family reunions every other year, and my mother and I would attend. Which relative was hosting determined the location—Bradenton, Florida, San Francisco, or Los Angeles. Momma Doe rarely attended, but my mother and Nana made sure we were there to meet more family. Because I carried my grandmother's name, it was easy to know from which elder I descended.

My father never traveled with us nor did he spend time with us during my weekend visits. He would come home from work at midnight and, like clockwork, eat dinner and return to the bedroom. We barely had conversations, even during breakfast together. One day, I asked him why he never accompanied us to the Broadway shows. He leaned over and replied, "Your mother pays to see them work in the day; I hang out with them for free at night." I was too afraid to ask him to explain, so I kept eating. While I was too young to comprehend his response, I recognized the look of shock on my mother's face. He called me into the bedroom the next day, asked me a few questions about school and my weekend, then gave me money. Sunday afternoon, Nana and I were on the Greyhound bus returning home.

After most visits with my parents in New York, I returned to Boston with a suitcase full of new designer clothing. More importantly, I experienced something cultural and exciting during these visits while deepening my relationship with my mother and Nana.

I was living a double lifestyle. As I got older, I began enjoying it even more. Eventually, I could travel to Manhattan alone. Noticing the increase in visits, my mother asked if I wanted to come live with her. She suggested that I could enroll in a boarding school and move to New York permanently. The idea was not appealing. It meant leaving my family and friends in Boston and still not living with my parents. In addition to my parents, other family also lived in New York. Aunt Eleanor and Uncle Lyle lived in Queens. They were really cousins, but in our family, if anyone was older, you called them aunt or uncle. Aunt Eleanor and Uncle Lyle had grandchildren, of which the oldest and I shared the same birthdate and often celebrated together.

Nonetheless, I would miss my Nana, my friends, and my cousins in Boston too much. Besides, I was experiencing the best of both worlds and did not want to lose that perceived luxury. When I asked my mother about her education, she told me that Nana enrolled her in a private school in Boston, and she had a broad and stimulating education. That explained why she called Nana, Dell and not mother. As a young girl, I loved having two mothers. But as an adult looking back on that conversation, my mother should have just made the motherly decision and made me move to New York. I was too young to understand the value of a private school versus a public school education.

Most weekends when visiting my mother, we saw two movies in the same day—one movie would be my choice, and she always selected the newest "007" James Bond movie. James Bond was interesting because he lived a double life as a top-secret British agent and his undercover role. My mother and I debated which James Bond actor was better—Sean Connery or Roger Moore. In addition to seeing movies, we also dined at fine restaurants on my weekend visits.

As my taste palette matured, my mother began broadening my exposure to a variety of foods. Meals included filet mignon and Lobster Thermador at any 5-star restaurant below 95th Street and especially on Manhattan's East Side. Because she grew up in private schools, my mother lacked the cooking skills of making soul food. We never ate a meal in Harlem and I was told not to walk past 100th Street. On one memorable occasion, we went to dinner at the Waldorf Astoria Hotel. The waiter suggested we try the Beef Wellington and a fresh steamed artichoke. This was the best meal I ever tasted. Savoring every bite, I begged my mother to cook this meal one day for me and teach me how to prepare it. My mother was so happy I enjoyed the meal we returned Sunday morning for brunch, and I ate my first omelet made fresh at the buffet table. Hours later, I boarded a Greyhound bus and headed back to Boston, my home base, my roots.

The week afterward was normal, except this time, at 12 years old, I was different. My taste buds had changed. Sunday morning breakfast consisted of grits with a slice of government cheese, scrambled eggs, biscuits and thick-cut pork bacon. I enjoyed every bite. Momma Doe cooked dinner and the aroma traveled through the house. I peeked into the kitchen and saw the bowl of baked macaroni and cheese. Pigs' feet were cooking in the big stainless-steel pot, and fresh collard greens and neckbones simmered in another pot. My job was to make the cornbread before we sat down for dinner. As I put food on my plate, I purposely did not get pigs' feet.

"Dell, you missed the pigs' feet," Charlene said, as I sat down.

I looked up and interrupted the flow of dinner as I stuttered. "I d-d-d-don't eat pigs' feet anymore."

The kitchen was quiet. You could hear a pin drop.

"Well, I am not cooking anything else," Momma Doe said as she turned her head all the way around. "You better eat what's on your plate, or you don't eat."

I was too spoiled to realize the value of my life. Both lifestyles were rewarding and would shape my life. But that Sunday, I ate all my food and Momma Doe never mentioned it again, nor did she ever prepare an alternative meat.

After dinner that Sunday, Momma Doe reminded us we were traveling to New Haven, Connecticut for the weekend and needed to make sure our bags were packed and chores completed Friday night.

My older sister JoAnn and her husband Roger had moved to New Haven with their four children, Roger, Norris, Nichelle and Tanya. On the weekends I was not in New York, I traveled with my family to New Haven. JoAnn and Roger had purchased a two-family house on Winchester Avenue. This trip was different because the family was planning Charlene's wedding. As a junior in high school, Charlene met the son of one of Roger's friends. After dating for almost a year, they were planning a wedding.

Charlene got married in September and moved out to live with her husband in New Haven. Now both sisters were in the same city, giving Momma Doe more reasons to visit New Haven. Although I was excited about the wedding, I was looking forward to starting high school and having the bedroom to myself. Home was great, I was the only child at home, and Momma Doe and I laughed and talked more. Yes, she did love me but showed it differently.

However, a few months after Charlene married, two young brothers, who were our cousins and had been bounced around from different family homes, joined our family. Everyone was committed to keeping the boys together and in the family. So the two brothers came to live with Momma Doe and me. We all had different last names, different parents but were family. I now had cousins who I called my brothers, and I was their sister.

FOUR THE HARD WAY

It was Labor Day in 1976, the long weekend before the first week of high school. My mother arranged for me to come to New York to go shopping before school started. I arrived in New York as usual. This time I was traveling by myself and had a big empty suitcase to bring back all of my new clothes. The Greyhound bus was three hours late, and I was hungry. I was fashionably dressed in hip-hugger blue jeans, a blue bodysuit, an Afro-pic hair comb with the Black power sign on top in the back of my head, and a bright yellow 4-inch belt. I didn't have much of a shapely figure; I was 5-feet, 2-inches, and looked like 6 o'clock, straight up and down. My clothes mirrored the dancers on Soul Train. It is what all the Black teenagers wore in Boston.

I stood at the station doorway looking for my mother. There she was, but it was like she was staring at me but did not recognize me. I said, "Mom, it's me" and was met by a look of horror on her face. She did not greet me with her normal smile. She didn't call me Pumpkin. She didn't even ask me if I was hungry. All she said was get your bags and follow me. She seemed embarrassed to be walking with me because she walked four steps ahead of me versus holding my hand while asking me about my trip and if I was excited about starting high school. The Greyhound bus was later than normal, and it was a little dark. As we rode the escalators upstairs I noticed that people looked different at Grand Central station, and it seemed busier than before. I assumed my mother was tired after working all day. She hurried us out of the station, swiftly walking to the corner of 42nd Street where she hailed a Yellow Cab. We got in the cab and headed to 100th Street between Amsterdam and Columbus. We weren't going out to eat, as usual. No, we were going home.

Once in the apartment, my mother immediately went into the kitchen and started cooking. I turned on the radio and started listening to station WBLS 107.5 FM and dancing in the living room. The DJ played James Brown's "I'm Black and I'm Proud," K.C. and the Sunshine Band, and some Parliament Funkadelic. My mother walked into the living room and turned down the radio.

"You do not want the neighbors to complain that you are playing your music too loud and tell your father," she said. "He will be home soon."

That is when I knew something was wrong. My father was never home before midnight. My mother made my favorite meal—filet mignon broiled medium-rare, French fries, tossed salad without onions and fresh iced tea. During dinner, when I asked her what was wrong, she looked at me with sad eyes and told me about a change of plans for the next day.

"Instead of going clothes shopping tomorrow, I made a hairdresser's appointment for you at 9 a.m.," she said. "When I saw you getting off the bus, I was scared. You looked like all the other young Black teenagers hanging around Grand Central station, and I was afraid that I could not keep you safe. I did not want someone to mistake you for someone else and approach you the wrong way.

"You have never been in Times Square at night. The people are different than the crowds during the day and I was scared for you. That is why I made sure that we got out of there very quickly, and I got you home."

Then my mother began to lecture me about having an Afro and a pic in the back of my head, wearing platform shoes and a bright yellow belt. She said I looked "unpolished" and "not like my daughter." It was the beginning of a lecture about dress perception and making sure that I was neat, polished and kept a clean appearance.

"That is why we are going to get your hair done tomorrow. Then I'm going to buy you some different clothes for high school," she continued.

I was in a beauty shop on 89th and Broadway getting my first relaxer by 10 the next morning. I looked in the mirror while the lady rolled my clipped ends and could see my mother smiling from the rear. Afterward, we jumped in a cab and went straight to the garment district, where the salesman had already selected outfits for me to try on. Two hours later, my mother had charged over $500 for outfits from Ann Taylor and Oleg Cassini, Ralph Lauren Polo sweaters, and Joan and David shoes. This time she had one of the ladies show me how to coordinate and arrange my clothes so that I could mix and match the colors to be a stylish teenager. After leaving the fashion district, we walked two blocks and picked out some leather boots to match the clothes I purchased. By the end of the day, I was exhausted. My curls had fallen from trying on all the clothes, but my hair was still straight. Sunday, we spent most of the day at the Guggenheim Museum on 5th Avenue and the Museum of Modern Art on 53rd Street between Fifth and Sixth avenues. My mother, looking at me, pointed out naked women, topless women, and silhouettes of women, and said "Art."

This weekend was the first stressful weekend visiting my mother in New York. I was looking forward to catching the bus back to Boston and starting high school. However, she made me promise to wear my clothes and avoid looking like most teenagers.

"You don't want someone to mistake you for someone else," she said.

When I returned home to Boston, Momma Doe picked me up from the bus station. We never discussed my new look. As a teenager, the quiet ride home bothered me. I silently wondered if she missed me and didn't know what to say about my drastic change and extra luggage or just didn't care. Momma Doe did not utter a word. I felt like a distant relative and not a daughter returning home. Either way, the silence was piercing and noticeable.

The first day of school was exciting as I walked the halls as a stylish teen with curled hair. I wore a pair of creased designer jeans, a Polo pullover V-neck sweater, and blue high-heel pumps. Sarah was a junior and for the first time I was introduced as her little sister. No one cared we had different last names and didn't resemble one another. I was called, "Sarah's little sister." I lived in her shadow. We arrived at school together and rode the city bus home sitting next to each other.

By the end of my freshman year, I established relationships with my own friends and no longer needed to be Sarah's little sister. Cindy and I met in 7th grade and grew closer as freshmen in high school. Later we met Robin, who joined our crew. By the next school year, Sarah was a senior and began playing basketball, and that's when I met Angel. People said she was from one of the toughest projects in Boston—Orchard Park—and that meant you didn't mess with her. Soon, we all forged a bond and were always together. Angel and I were in the same homeroom. Although not related, because their last names were Johnson, Cindy and Robin were in the same homeroom.

I began traveling to Manhattan with these new high school friends rather than Sarah. They were exposed to my other lifestyle in New York and we loved it. We spent our sophomore year attending basketball and football games, parties in the gym after school and weekends at Cindy's or Robin's house because their mothers allowed us to stay the longest, make the most noise, play spades, practice the latest dance steps, and enjoy being teenagers. Because we were always together, one of the football players began calling us "Four the Hard Way." We had a sisterly friendship bond that has lasted a lifetime.

During a return trip from visiting my mother, Robin and I wrote a chant entitled "Four the Hard Way," We sang that song throughout high school and into adulthood.

FOUR THE HARD WAY
Our name is Robin, Cindy, Angel, and Odell,
we go to Tech, and they know us well.
They all know that we don't play,
Because Dixon calls us Four the Hard Way. Bada ba da.

The winter of our sophomore year, Four the Hard Way went skiing through a local city agency called Y.E.S.—Youth Enrichment Services. Angel was the only experienced skier, so they told us to take lessons before getting on the lift. I must have missed those instructions. Coming off the lift I ran my skis into Robin's back while she was practicing. We decided the outdoor life was not for Four the Hard Way. Instead, we returned to spending weekends in New York with my mother as a great escape from Boston. On one of our visits, my mother rented a hotel room in Times Square because Sarah joined us this time and the apartment was too small for five teenagers. She purchased tickets to see the Broadway show *Eubie* starring the famous Hines Brothers. *Eubie* was Angel's first Broadway show. My mother told us to stay together for safety because the environment changed and demanded that we return to the hotel directly after the show. Earlier that day, we lunched at a 4-star restaurant and shopped in the garment district. We felt like royalty, selecting dresses from the designer showcase.

After the show, Angel wanted to hang around the stage door and get Gregory Hines' autograph. Robin, Cindy, Sarah, and I preferred to follow my mother's directive and return to the hotel. Times Square looked intimidating at night. People were selling everything—sex, drugs, and X-rated movies. This was my first time in Times Square alone; it seemed like a different place. Angel was mad we did not want to stay with her, and she left us standing outside the theater. We turned our heads, and she was gone. So, we walked back to the hotel and nervously waited for Angel to return. Hours later, we heard a knock at the door, and Angel resurfaced with a sketch she bought from a sidewalk artist. Although we were mad at her for days, we never told my mother. It took years for us to laugh at these events.

When I turned 16, my mother and I began traveling overseas. One benefit of my father working for TWA airline is that his family could travel on standby at no cost. My father did not join us on these trips. He was afraid of flying and once said he saw enough of the world when he was in the military. However, he helped to finance our travels. I would wake up on the morning we were scheduled to depart for our latest journey and find many $100 bills on the table with a note that said, "for the baby." My mother exchanged them for travelers' checks, and we were ready to go. My father accompanied us to the airport boarding area and let the flight attendant know we were his family. My mother had traveled so many times they knew her by name. In an infrequent display of fatherly affection, my father told the flight attendant to take care of his daughter. My mother just smiled as we boarded the plane.

Every summer, we traveled to two countries for three weeks—France, Italy, Greece, and England. My first trip was to Paris. That summer before leaving I met a popular high school basketball player, Alonzo. He asked for my number so he could call the next day. I told him I would not be home the next day as I was going to Paris, France, for the summer. He gave me a look of disbelief.

"If you don't want to talk to me, just say no," he said. "You don't have to say you're going to Paris. What Black girl living in Dorchester on the Four Corners goes to Paris for the summer?"

He gave me his address and telephone number and rode away on his bike, saying sarcastically, "Find me when you return."

When I returned in late August, he was dating a girl in his neighborhood. We sat on his steps and shared details of my vacation, talking and laughing for hours. He was the first male teenager who seemed genuinely interested and intrigued by my travels and my double lifestyle. And I gave him a bottle of French cologne. The postcard I sent him arrived weeks later. Although we couldn't date, it was the beginning of a great friendship.

In my junior year of high school, I was the first person in our Four the Hard Way group to receive my driver's license, and I was probably the worst driver. Angel's mother rented a car for us to go out, making me promise not to let anyone drive except me—the license holder. We went to a club that night. In my first attempt to back down a dark street, I hit ten parked cars. Then I tried to park between two cars and ran into a parked car. The owner was mad because he was trying to change his tire. After we left the club, Angel took the keys and refused to let me drive anymore. My excuse was that this was my first time driving at night. We laughed all night long and told Angel's mother that someone must have hit the car. My sister Sarah had already graduated from Boston Tech and decided to take a year off before attending college. She was in the car with us when I hit all those parked cars. The next day she wrote this poem:

ODE TO ODELL
Well, Well, Well, if it ain't Odell,
Here she comes and looking well,
Creased blue jeans, pumps, and a "T,"
with her nickname, which reads O period D.
O.D is my sister, as you all know,
I'm very proud of her; she's my prize to show,
She rented a car, Brought it back with a dent,
But she's Miss International; she's been from continent to continent.
She travels all over; she's never at home,
She's been to Greece, Italy, Mexico, and Rome,
Be as it may, Be as it might,
My sister and I are truly a delight,

With Grace, charm, and taste to start,
She'll always have a place in my heart,
No one can measure to her, to me
Love to my sister Odell as O.D.

My mother arranged for Robin, Angel, and me to travel to Rome during spring break that year. Cindy was now the mother of a beautiful little girl and could not leave the country, so we brought her back a special gift. Culturally, it was an eye-opener for my friends. The men in Rome were fascinated and confused about our race. Robin's auburn colored hair and light skin, Angel had a light brown complexion with black hair, and I had the darkest skin color. They could not determine our ethnicity. The bartender kept giving Robin bottles of free alcohol every night. We were not old enough to drink and were the only Black American girls in the hotel. So, the hotel manager kept an eye out to make sure we were safe. A wealthy businessman staying at the hotel kept calling me "chocolate" and offered to take me back to Milan with him. A young man at the hotel drooled every time Angel came into the lobby. He must have touched her, but all we saw was her showing a fist, which is a universal language, and he never bothered her again. Robin walked by and said, "Orchard Park."

We spent a week in Rome being tourists, sightseeing the Colosseum, Vatican, Catacombs, Pompeii, and shopping. We saw the flirty businessman at the airport the day we left, and he stopped and offered to buy me an airline ticket. We didn't know anything about human trafficking or Americans being kidnapped. All I knew was that he was a rich, handsome Italian man wearing expensive clothes and exquisite shoes, interested in the dark-skinned skinny one—me. But I also knew not to go with this stranger. Our trip was memorable, and we talked about our trip for years. Angel and Robin brought gifts back for their families and something special for their brothers.

TWO BROTHERS

Once we landed back in New York, our bus was not returning to Boston for another two days. My mother wanted to hear all about our vacation. We conveniently left out the stories of the men and discussed our sightseeing and dining excursions. She was delighted to hear about our spring break and immediately took advantage of the opportunity to discuss our college plans. She made it clear we should not attend the same college and was adamant we should expand our horizons. While Angel and Robin showed their gifts for their brothers and our other purchases, I asked my mother for a brother. My mother glanced at my father who was eating lunch at the table. She calmly walked to the black phone in the hallway. I heard her dialing the rotary phone. After a pause, she said, "Hi Ben, it's Mary. Your sister Dell wants to meet you."

I was confused. Although my parents never had the sex talk with me, I knew placing a phone call was not how children were born. Much to my surprise, I discovered that my father had been previously married and had two sons living in Williamsburg, Virginia. So, before I graduated from high school, I flew to Virginia to meet them.

Ben and Montez were 18 and 17 years older than me, respectively. By the time we met, their mother was a retired schoolteacher and had only exchanged conversations with my mother via phone. She had pleasant words about my mother, as my mother sent money and clothes during the winter when the boys were growing up. She did not hesitate to welcome me into the family and immediately called me her daughter.

It was a great week sitting at the kitchen table, feeling like I was complete. These guys were not my cousins, whom I was calling my brothers. I did not care that my brothers knew about me and did not attempt to connect with me. I was elated because we shared similar interests, behaviors, and characteristics. Ben resembled our father more, while Montez, at 6-feet tall, shared our father's height. Montez was stricken with polio as a child, and his right arm was underdeveloped. He wore big green glasses; my glasses were red. I now knew where my sense of color and style originated. I also had a nephew—Ben named his son Duke Benjamin Montgomery III, but they called him Monty.

In his mother's living room, I saw articles about Montez playing

tennis with tennis legend Arthur Ashe. I was so proud to have brothers! Montez was a Ph.D. candidate at Kent State University in Ohio. I
left Virginia expecting to achieve greatness. Being a Montgomery had
a new meaning.

"I don't believe in half-sister language. You are my sister, and I
am your brother," Montez said. "You are a Montgomery, so carry the
name in class."

I didn't know what that meant, but it felt good. When I returned
to Boston, my behavior was different. I felt validated.

As I moved into my senior year in high school, my home life in
Boston was going through a transition. Sarah had decided to stay
home and work before attending college. Charlene was now divorced
and living in the house with her boyfriend. Their room was across
from mine. The brothers shared a room, Momma Doe's room was at
the end of the hallway, and Nana had a room on the first floor. I began resenting all my years of restrictions and being told what I could
not do. I could only have boy company after I was 16 years old, and
they could only come to the house on Sunday after 4 p.m. and leave
by 10 p.m. No phone calls were allowed from anyone, girl or boy,
after 10 p.m. When I went to a party with my friends, my curfew
was still 12:30 a.m. I was the only one dancing like the girls on Soul
Train because I had to leave before everyone else and I was gonna get
my dance on. The curfew didn't seem fair, especially with Charlene
having a boyfriend living in the house. The older teens in the neighborhood had nicknamed me Cinderella. I was getting off the city bus
to go home while they were just leaving to go out. In the summer,
we would stay on the porch or hang out in Sarah's room. One thing
remained unchanged. After completing my chores on Friday, I was on
a Greyhound bus headed to New York with a round-trip ticket.

I graduated from high school in 1980. Momma Doe did not attend my 8th grade or high school graduations. Because of her absence
from my high school graduation, I questioned if she was proud of me
or upset because I decided to live with my mother and attend college

in New York. Charlene, Sarah, my mother, Nana and Darsweil, a cousin from California, were present. Although Charlene and I ignored each other in the house, I knew she loved me. In my opinion, we had developed this love-hate relationship. Now that we were older, it was easier to identify it and keep moving. Unfortunately, it still felt empty not having Momma Doe present again. I never asked, and she never explained her absence.

ONE WAY TICKET PLEASE

I was accepted into Pratt Institute in Brooklyn, New York, majoring in Nutrition and Dietetics. Angel stayed home and attended Brandeis University, and Robin went to Syracuse University in Syracuse, New York. Cindy stayed in Boston to be a mother to her daughter.

Against my mother's advice, I moved into a co-ed dorm at Pratt with four roommates. The two White students selected the larger room, and I shared the smaller room with a Black girl from Niagara Falls, New York. The campus was small and multi-cultural. All the Black students who did not commute lived in the co-ed dorm. Living on campus in Brooklyn was great. I met new friends who often teased me about my Boston accent. I would ask if we could go to a party; they thought I said, "potty." In high school, I was barely allowed to attend parties. When I was permitted to go, I had a curfew. I was always the first person sneaking out of a party. Living between Brooklyn and Manhattan was phenomenal. I wanted to attend all the clubs.

In the city, the clubs didn't close until daybreak. I partied at Studio 54 and the Garage Club. Walking out of the clubs when the sun was up was strange, but I loved it. Other than my roommates, I bonded quickly with the others living in the dorm. Most of my friends were athletes and from Brooklyn. Two basketball players introduced themselves by knocking on my dorm door one day and telling me, "We smell food in here. Can we come in?" They came in, and we connected immediately. It was easier to meet guys when you weren't scheming to date them. I focused on my freshman year academics. I learned the importance of financial aid and a minimum 3.0 grade point average.

By the time Thanksgiving arrived, I was headed to the city to spend time with my mother. Unbeknownst to me, my mother had separated from my father and moved to an apartment two blocks away from the apartment they shared. All my life, I remembered coming into New York and arriving at 100th Street between Amsterdam and Columbus Avenue. This was a major change. I was curious about why my mother insisted on meeting in Times Square for dinner first. During our meal, my mother informed me that she left my father, and we had a new apartment on Central Park and 110th. Since she had moved just down the street, the move did not make much sense to me at the time.

After dinner, we caught a cab to our new apartment. It didn't feel like home.

My parents always had a one-bedroom apartment, and I slept on the pull-out couch in the living room. Now that my mother had moved, I wondered if I would have my own room. Walking into my mother's new apartment for the first time, I noticed a new couch in the living room and the one bedroom in the back. She said that I did not need my own room since I lived on campus. Either way, my sleeping arrangements had not changed.

I pulled out the couch and went to sleep in my new home. This apartment had all-white walls and seemed hollow. I did not like the apartment; it didn't feel lived in or warm. We had Thanksgiving dinner in Queens with our family, and Sunday afternoon, I caught the train back to campus.

At Pratt, I was awarded work-study and began working in the athletics department. The men's basketball team had low attendance at their games because of their inconsistent winning record. The newly hired athletic director asked if I could assist him with creating a cheerleader squad to increase attendance at athletic events. The director was a nice man, so I began my first attempt at organizing. I ordered candy to sell during the Colgate Track Meet that Pratt hosted and recruited other students in the dorm to assist. Using the money we raised, we ordered black pom-poms and black and gold V-neck sweaters. The director recruited a woman in a sorority, and she taught us some chants. We cheered and chanted in the stands during the basketball games, and people started attending. The players liked to hear us calling their names.

On the weekends, I would practice cooking new nutritious dishes and invite my friends over as tasters. Tony was my closest friend at Pratt; we made a friendship pack: whenever I got married and had children, he would be the godfather.

After my freshman year, I returned to Manhattan and slept on the couch. My mother made me work and volunteer; she said it developed character. One weekend, between my jobs, I went home to Boston. Nana had retired and was living with Momma Doe. Sarah and her mother still lived on the first floor of the two-family house, and she had started college and was barely home. Momma Doe adopted some children, and they were now living in my bedroom. All my school pictures were gone. I had to sleep with Nana in her double bed. When I walked into her room, there on the dresser or wall were every picture I took from 1st grade to high school. I walked over to Nana sitting in her rocking chair and gave her a big kiss. We talked about school, and she asked me to please graduate college before she died.

"I am hanging on to see that day of you in your cap and gown," she said.

Home did not seem like my home anymore. Alonzo, Angel, and Robin happened to be home the same weekend, and we connected before I drove back to campus. We didn't know where Cindy was living. We lost contact during my college years. Eventually, I stopped returning to Boston. The boys were finishing high school and were always either at work or at their friends' houses. Boston did not seem like my home anymore. I felt as if I had been erased.

Sunday morning, I drove back home to Manhattan because I had to work on Monday.

One guy on the Pratt track team was dating a girl named Val, a student at NYU (New York University). Eventually, Val and I developed a great friendship. We began hanging out in the city instead of Brooklyn. One summer night after work, she suggested we walk to Harlem and have dinner. Although I lived on 95th Street and was 19 years old, I was too afraid to tell Val that I had never walked to

Harlem, nor had I ever eaten in Harlem. I followed her lead and we laughed and talked the entire walk, but I was scared. My mother's voice was echoing in my head, "Never walk past 100th Street. It's no man's land." When we arrived at the soul food restaurant, she ordered fried chicken, yams, macaroni and cheese, and cabbage. I ordered a cheeseburger and proceeded to cut my burger in half. I noticed the strange look on her face, but she remained silent.

After our fourth trip to Harlem, Val scolded me.

"Why do you always order a burger and then cut it with your knife? Will you please order some real soul food?"

It was then I had to confess that I had never ordered soul food in a restaurant in New York. I explained my life with my mother, the chef, and being told never to walk to Harlem. She finally understood why I ordered the burgers. Before leaving I ordered the soul food special to go. When I reached my mother's apartment, I warmed up the chicken in the oven for a late-night snack. Smelling the aroma, my mother came out of the room. I had to share my meal with her, and she ate most of it. She assumed because I was with Val, her mother cooked. My mother wiped her mouth, said it was delicious and went back to her room. I felt like I was sitting in Momma Doe's kitchen eating dinner. I could not understand why my mother prohibited me from going to Harlem. All the jazz clubs and good food were in Harlem. My father had it right all these years. Harlem!

Occasionally, Alonzo's college played basketball against teams in New York or neighboring New Jersey. He always called ahead of the games and made sure I had tickets. We would make eye contact while he was playing and have a quick visit before his coach rushed all the players on the bus to head back to campus. When Angel and Robin came to New York for a visit, we had new places to visit, now Harlem was on the agenda. We partied Friday night at Studio 54 and heard Taana Gardner perform her latest R&B hit, "Heartbeat," at a jazz club in Harlem. Then Saturday, we went to another club in lower Manhattan. After dancing all night, we walked into the back room and noticed actor Calvin Lockhart playing chess.

We found a seat and stared at him all night long. We were three star-struck women. Lockhart was a handsome man and played chess with style. It was daybreak when we left, but we were taking advantage of the free time on spring break. After sleeping late, we ate the delicious breakfast my mother made before packing our bags and sitting outside her house, waiting for Robin's ride. We laughed and reminisced about our weekend and how much we were enjoying college and life. When Robin's ride arrived, instead of saying goodbye, she invited Angel and me to join her at Syracuse. Angel and I looked at each other and jumped in the back seat of the car for our first trip to Syracuse University. We laughed the entire trip, thinking about what I was going to tell my mother. In the '80s, we did not have cellphones, email or text messages, so I had to wait until I arrived in Syracuse to phone my mother about my change in plans. She laughed and said, "Have fun!" When I returned, I went straight to campus to avoid sleeping on the couch in our apartment.

I didn't know it at the time, but I would not return to the apartment. Months later, I visited my mother at a new apartment on 95th and Central Park West, four blocks away from my father's house. What did she love about this neighborhood, and why was I never included in selecting the apartment? I rode the elevator to the 14th floor and walked into a one-bedroom apartment with the same couch. This time, there was a wall closet for my clothes and a dresser in the living room. My mother hung her artwork and purchased a room divider to provide me with some privacy. The albums must have been my father's because I did not see them in the new apartment. My mother had expensive wines in her small wine rack. Since she did not drink, I took the wine back to my dorm. I was the only student in college with a wine rack in the dorm filled with $100 bottles of the best wines. I learned early to develop a taste for Bordeaux.

We had the corner apartment, 14B, which was a little better. You could smell everyone's cooking on the floor. Our neighbor was Latino and was always cooking something tasty. My mother had retired from her position as the chef for a bank on Wall Street. And although she was still on retainer for several families on the upper east side of Manhattan, she told me that the rent was better in this apartment.

Being a chef meant my mother worked some holidays. She was catering a Thanksgiving dinner for a family and hired me along with my cousin to wash the dishes. My pay was $200. The client came into the kitchen and told my mother that the children's nanny was sick. She wanted to hire me as the children's nanny for the day. Because it was short notice and the holiday, she offered to pay me $650 for the day. I quickly threw my apron in the chair and left my mother and cousin in the kitchen. Later that day, they had to serve me. It was annoying sitting at the children's table and being ignored by the adults while listening to their conversations, but I kept thinking about earning $650 in one day.

CHAPTER 2
INTERRUPTION: A DIFFERENT WORLD

MY COUSIN DARSWEIL AND I MET when I was ten years old during a family visit to Los Angeles, California. A Howard University graduate, he lived around the corner from Pratt and worked on Wall Street. The family in New York extended the red carpet to him and made sure he was fed and comfortable during this new phase of his life after college. Our home became his home away from home. One night I invited him to campus for dinner in exchange for help with my accounting project. I thought he would be impressed with my popularity. Instead, as we walked back to his apartment to hang out, he shared a startling observation.

"Cuz, this school is underutilizing your full potential. If you remain at Pratt, I think you will be wasting your life," he said.

I was confused by his comment. My friends were athletes and active in the Black Student Union, and I was active in the Nutrition Club. His comment was like a dagger to my ego. How did my struggle with my accounting project equate to me wasting my life? After debating with him for the next 10 minutes, Darsweil would not change his opinion. He insisted that we visit Howard University (HU) in Washington, D.C., during spring break. Two months later, we left Brooklyn and the quiet campus of Pratt Institute and drove three hours to D.C.

I noted that the HU students wore designer blue jeans and penny loafers, silk dresses, and pumps. I was no longer on Pratt's campus. I wondered whether this was the norm and what I had been missing.

Darsweil escorted me to the section of The Yard—a designation for the main campus—where his fraternity brothers from the Alpha Phi Alpha fraternity were stepping. He joined them in the next step and did not miss a footstep, a spoken word, or the rather complex turn or jump. Was this my cousin? Who was this man? Is this the same man I saw returning from work on Wall Street? All I could do was stand among the crowd and look on in amazement. I cheered with the other students and laughed when they did. But I really had no idea what the steppers were saying. My curiosity was heightened by the other crowds on The Yard. I casually strolled the green space, trying not to appear out of place, but was amazed at the noon-day activities. Every corner of the Howard University Yard offered a different energy from the sororities and fraternities there. Arriving on the Howard University campus felt like I was on another planet.

I had never seen that many Black college students in one location in my entire life. The fraternities and sororities were gathered in designated areas on The Yard and were "stepping." This was my first time observing people step. Stepping is a form of dance in which the fraternity or sorority members use their bodies as instruments to produce complex rhythms and sounds through a mixture of footsteps, spoken word, calls and responses, and hand claps. It is generally performed by three or more people, often in arrangements that resemble military formations. The students who were watching the performances laughed and cheered. Each of the Divine 9 fraternities and sororities had distinguished colors, paraphernalia (shields, red and white candy canes, ducks, elephants) and each had a unique hand signal. It was slick and impressive.

Hours later the crowds dispersed and Darsweil took me to Howard Hospital for lunch. I thought to myself, "Who voluntarily eats food at a hospital?" Much to my surprise, I proceeded to devour some of the best fried chicken and collard greens I'd eaten since living in Boston. It was Darsweil's mission to show me the best of HU. Thus far, I was sold.

Saturday morning, he insisted we eat at the Florida Avenue Grill, a small diner with limited seating. Again, I prejudged the diner based on the outward appearance, thinking that my mother would never have been seen eating there. This place looked worse than the restaurant in Harlem. Again, I was ordering soul food at a restaurant, this time in the hood in D.C. I recalled the brunch with my mother at the Waldorf-Astoria in New York. Darsweil noticed my face was frowning. He knew my childhood. His father was a medical doctor, and they grew up with a maid.

"In college, you don't use your parents' credit card; you have to adjust and eat what you can afford, trust me!" he said, leaning down to look me in the eyes. "You will love it."

When the food arrived, Darsweil asked my thoughts. As a culinary student and the daughter of Mary Montgomery the chef, was it possible that the grits, bacon, biscuits and eggs were better than Momma Doe's? The Florida Avenue Grill food was the bomb!

Darsweil gave me a guided tour of the campus, including the School of Human Ecology. If I transferred, this would be the school that housed my major. Then we walked toward the science buildings, and I learned these buildings were referred to as "Death Valley." The name made me shudder.

The day ended in the Blackburn Building student center, eating more fried chicken and shooting pool in the game room. Fine, articulate Black men of all hues and politeness filled the room. If this was the HBCU experience, sign me up! The entire weekend was one new breath-taking experience after another. I was concerned the school would ask for a picture before I was admitted. Most women were fashionably dressed, wore high heels, and had immaculate perms and flawless makeup. I wondered whether what I observed was the expected manner of dress to be accepted into Howard University.

Monday morning, I walked into the Administration Building of Howard University; the 'A Building' is what the students called it. I submitted my application and agreed to provide my transcripts upon returning to Pratt.

After my visit to Howard, the Pratt campus was not the same. Quiet and uneventful, it wasn't easy enjoying the campus life, although the weekends were still phenomenal clubbing in the city.

Months later, I learned I was accepted as a transfer student into the Howard University School of Human Ecology for the Fall of 1982. My mother was a firm believer that I should continue my studies in nutrition and dietetics and become a registered dietitian. She said the field was promising, and an educated Black woman would be highly pursued and compensated in this field, especially as a graduate of Howard University. I did not argue with my mother's choice. Studying nutrition and dietetics at Pratt was not overly exciting, but she was paying my tuition. The science classes were harder and really didn't have my full interest. I was passing with a low B- and I found myself excelling in the cooking and management classes. I quickly learned very few Black women were hired as registered dieticians; therefore, they would become highly employable. I was committed to working hard at what my mother felt would be a lucrative career path once I graduated because my mother said so, and she was rarely wrong.

As I was preparing to leave for Howard to begin the fall semester of 1982, my mother helped me pack the car and told me to drive safely and call her when I arrived. Instead of immediately driving to D.C., I stayed the weekend in Brooklyn with my friends from Pratt to party one last time before leaving the next morning.

DREAMS ON HOLD

I arrived at the party but left to pick up a friend who needed a ride. What seemed like moments later, I heard people calling my name. "Odell! Odell wake up! Wake up!" I could barely open my eyes, and everything seemed blurry. I heard voices in the room say, "Her mother and family are on the way." Hours later, I learned that a drunk driver ran a red light and slammed into my side of the car, pinning me behind the wheel of my Plymouth Horizon. I was put in an ambulance and sent to the Brooklyn Hospital.

I remained in the hospital for two weeks suffering from eleven fractured ribs, collapsed lungs, and damage to my knees. August 28—the date of the accident—is a day I will never forget. Instead of being a transfer student at Howard University, starting a new chapter in my education, I recuperated at home sleeping on the pullout couch.

I spent the entire semester, from August to January, six months, with my mother flat on my back. I had not previously spent so much time in the apartment or anywhere, for that matter, with my mother. Before the accident, I was only home for weekends and two or three months in the summer. I could not remember ever seeing my mother angry, and she never spanked me. Mary had a calm spirit and never raised her voice. But lying on the bed, barely breathing, with limited mobility, I wondered when my mother was going to yell at me for lying to her about my whereabouts. I felt guilty that I disappointed her and wondered how she would show her anger or relief.

Instead of anger, my mother cooked all my favorite meals for breakfast, lunch, and dinner for the next three months and helped me shower. Every night we watched my favorite TV shows, most of which she hated. My mother clipped my nails and moisturized my feet. She enjoyed lecturing me on the importance of a woman keeping her hands and feet manicured and soft. She hired a hairdresser to wash and braid my hair. It was her pet peeve to see me unkempt, regardless of how much pain I was feeling. The hospital gave me a breathing device to strengthen my lungs. The goal was to blow enough air into the device until the three balls raised to the top of the one-inch chamber. I practiced ten times a day with no success in moving a ball, but I was determined.

My doctor said I could walk on my own once I moved all three balls consistently for one week. My nights were painful. I could barely breathe and only slept on my back. The mattress on the couch was thin and uncomfortable. When my friends visited, my mother cooked them a culinary meal to rival a five-star restaurant. She even uncorked an expensive bottle of wine for them to enjoy without me. I began to wonder if my friends were coming to see me or eat my mother's food. They talked about life at Pratt without my cooking and gave me updates. It hurt to laugh, but it felt good to have company. After dinner, my mother cleaned the kitchen and retired to her room, giving us privacy. Once my friends left, my mother would kiss me on the forehead and say, "Good night, Pumpkin, I love you." I guess she was relieved I was alive because she never mentioned that I lied to her about my whereabouts the night of the accident.

I was totally dependent on my mother to be my caretaker. At times I wished she would fuss at me instead of lecturing me about caring for my body and hair. Some nights we played short games of Scrabble, which she always won, or Hearts. Occasionally, she had a private catering event for a family on the eastside. She cooked my dinner and left it on the stove. When she returned, she cleaned the kitchen and kissed me on my forehead, and said, "Good night, Pumpkin, I love you."

Every day, I continued to blow into my breathing device and slowly began making progress. On the day that I could finally muster a breath strong enough to move all three balls in the chamber, I was so excited. The next morning, I awoke and pushed in the couch. When my mother came into the living room, I made us a cup of hot tea and fresh fruit. She smiled and gave me a big hug. I let out a loud cry because I was not completely healed. Laughing, she instructed me to return to the couch and rest, assuring me that I was not returning to school that semester.

One night she cooked dinner for Darsweil and discussed my health and school with him. During their conversation, he recommended she call the dean at Howard University to request incomplete grades for all my fall classes. I would avoid receiving failing grades in all my courses, and I could keep my financial aid. My mother followed Darsweil's advice, and the dean approved the request. I would still have to complete the 18 credits from the fall and enroll for another 14 credits in the spring to remain a full-time student. According to Darsweil, I had to earn 32 credit hours in one semester! But he was confident I could do it!

I spent the next two months building my lungs and walking around the neighborhood to gain my strength. My mother secured a lawyer and filed a lawsuit against the driver. As a result, all of my medical bills were paid, and I received enough money to buy another car. However, my mother was uncomfortable with me driving again and decided to delay buying me a new car until the following year. There it was, finally, my punishment. We went to New Haven, and Roger and JoAnn helped us pick out a new '83 black Chevrolet. However, the car stayed in JoAnn and Roger's driveway until my mother gave them permission to let me have it.

When the spring semester began, I was medically cleared to return to school. I was still sore and not walking with vigor, but I was determined to resume my education. I returned to Howard, selecting classes that did not require written essays because it was difficult to type and sit upright in chairs. While standing in the registration line for classes, I overheard students discussing the Public Speaking-Communications class and how it was an easy three credits. Being an impetuous student, I registered for the course. Upon arriving for class in Locke Hall on a sunny Friday afternoon, I noticed the class was filled with upperclassmen, mostly Omega Psi Phi and Alpha Phi Alpha fraternity men. It appeared all the students knew one another and showed reverence toward one particular fraternity brother in Omega Psi Phi. I later learned that his name was Jerome Peters. A tall and slim medical student, Jerome was the most popular student in the class. He wore a fraternity shirt with blue jeans and nice shoes to every class.

I immediately felt invisible, and my confidence in the possibility of earning a passing grade disappeared abruptly. The professor reviewed the course syllabus with us and discussed our final class project, a 10-minute presentation. I had an entire semester to build my confidence and to decide on a topic to present. When the professor circulated the sign-up sheet, I proudly placed my name on the last day and time slot for a presentation. I was hoping that most of the students would be absent or leave class early on the last day.

I always arrived early to class and secured the seat next to the door. I barely spoke unless the professor called my name. I continued to feel invisible and was no longer excited about being an HU student. What was I thinking? Did I make a mistake in transferring? At Pratt, I was popular and had friends. During my freshman year, I had a pajama party that lasted all weekend. My mother cooked a huge pot of shrimp gumbo and provided cases of Golden Champale. I was known and respected. Now, here I was in my first class at HU, and no one knew my name or realized that I existed.

I was still recovering from the collapsed lungs, so breathing and walking were difficult. However, I submitted my assignments on time, and I had perfect attendance. Therefore, if I scored low points on the class presentation, my attendance and other assignments should provide me with a passing grade. My grades were good in the other classes, and I felt optimistic about passing this semester except for the communications class. The semester went by extremely fast, and before I knew it, the date for the presentation was just two weeks away. The other students had used overhead projectors and handouts, presenting with confidence and clarity. The professor graded students at the end of each presentation before they returned to their seats. My fear was being embarrassed and ridiculed by the other students since I stuttered, and they didn't even know I existed. I struggled with finding a topic that would be captivating. My roommate was cool and tried to calm my nerves. We shared the same name—Odell. It was my first name and her last name—Sharon Odell. Sharon told me I would be fine and that I should imagine the audience with their clothes off. That image did not help my confidence since it was a room full of attractive and intelligent Black men.

After returning to my dorm from classes one day, I found a letter from my friend Angel and an article from a fashion magazine. The article suggested women enjoyed having their toes sucked. The article discussed Sigmund Freud's penis envy theory, suggesting women were envious of men. The basis of Sigmund Freud's female psychosexual development theory describes how women experience anxiety upon realizing that they do not have a penis. The article stated that women have only elongated fingers and toes; therefore, women are sexually aroused by having their toes sucked as a man is from his penis being sucked. This article was exciting. I spent days in the library research-ing this theory and reading the entire article in the journal. When I discussed it with my roommate and friends, they laughed so hard and had many questions. Then it dawned on me that this would be the article I would use for my class presentation. It was funny, intriguing, educational, and sparked curiosity.

I made copies of the article for handouts. During my work hours,

I surveyed 100 HU students who occasionally came into the game room at the Blackburn Center, where I was assigned work-study. While at work, I pitched my class topic and asked various students to participate in the experiment with their girlfriend or boyfriend. They had to report the results in three days, and I promised to keep their names anonymous. To my surprise, 90 percent of the students provided feedback. Some thanked me with a huge smile and free lunch, while others said, "Not for me."

On the last day of class and the last time slot, the professor called my name. My knees were shaking, and I hoped I would not stutter. Somehow, if I could engage the class early with laughter and smiles, it would minimize my stuttering. I remembered how I felt coming home and finding the Elton John record on my bed encouraging me to beat the odds. On presentation day my classmates were all present, watching me approach the center of the room. Jerome was sitting in the front row wearing another fraternity sweater. I thought, "How many purple and gold sweaters does this guy have?" It did not help that he was more handsome close-up. I immediately knew that picturing him naked would not be wise.

Finally, standing at the front of the room, I said, "My name is Odell Montgomery, and I want to talk about Sigmund Freud's theory of . . ." I saw the faces drop and eyes roll until I said, "Penis Envy Theory." Everyone sat up straight in their chairs, and I had their undivided attention. I shared Freud's premise and passed out copies of the article.

My presentation included information about Freud's theory and the results of my survey. The class was most impressed that I could recruit 100 students to participate in this exercise and voluntarily share the results. The students wanted to know more about the process: One toe or all the toes? Did they have to touch the feet or just the toes? The questions of intrigue and excitement kept coming. I could barely complete a sentence before another person interrupted with a thought and another intriguing question. Ten minutes flew by, and my time ended.

When finished, I glanced over at the professor sitting in the chair, mesmerized and shocked by my presentation. The professor took a deep breath and said that my presentation was unexpected. However, the class seemed engaged and interested in the presentation, and they had plenty of questions. I could see him glance at all the smiles and laughter in the class, and he gave me an A.

I passed all my classes for the spring and fall semesters and felt a huge sense of accomplishment. My brothers would tell me I was a Montgomery for motivation! By the summer, Mary gave me permission to pick up my car from New Haven. Then I became her taxi driver while I was home, and I never complained.

Once I returned to Howard, I received calls from my Aunt Eleanor and Nana that my mother fell and was in the hospital. The report was she was fine and didn't want me to come home.

That summer, Alonzo called to tell me that he was in Atlanta mourning the passing of his brother. I had never heard him sound so sad. I flew to Atlanta for the week and stayed at his mother's house. I wanted to be there to console my friend. During college, I attended his basketball games, and he visited me in Manhattan. He was one of my male friends that my mother liked and thought had a promising career. On this visit to Atlanta, his mother and I spent the day together while he ran personal errands with his friends. Alonzo and I were invited to his friend's house to play cards. We walked up a long driveway and a very tall man opened the door and welcomed us, motioning for us to make ourselves comfortable. I remember this guy turning on music with a remote control. "How cool was that?" I thought. I had never seen any sound system that advanced. Other men appeared, and they were all tall. Once everyone arrived, the host asked me if I played Spades. I thought, "I'm a Thompson, of course, I play cards." I did not remember any names, just that most of the guests were tall and good-looking Black men. Alonzo did not play cards but sat on the couch watching the basketball game. Once again, men and their sports. I felt surrounded by sports commentators. Everyone had a comment about a player, the referee, and the players' personality. We started playing Spades, and I was having fun. The night was fun, and my friend was smiling and laughing. I do not remember which NBA team was playing, but the guys at the house all seemed to know everything about the game. The next day, I headed back to D.C. Alonzo expressed his appreciation for my visit.

Near the end of the fall semester, I received another call that my mother was back in the hospital, but I didn't need to come home. This time, I completed all my exams and rode home early for Christmas. While waiting in the hospital lobby, the Knicks basketball game came on the television. As the game began, and the opposing team came out, I noticed the players on the Atlanta team looked familiar. Then I recognized another player. My mouth dropped. I was shocked. These were the guys I played cards with when I visited Alonzo in Atlanta. I had never felt more embarrassed and stupid. That explained why they were all tall and could comment on the game. They were professional NBA players. Later that week, I told Alonzo about my Christmas Day discovery. He just laughed and said, "I thought you knew."

Before returning to school, Aunt Eleanor finally broke her promise and told me my mother had cancer and was dying. She had been diagnosed with multiple myeloma the year I started college, which explained why she retired from Wall Street and found a one-bedroom rent-controlled apartment.

CELEBRATION OF LIFE FOR MARY!

I spent most of my free time during my junior year at Howard, traveling back and forth to New York. My mother tried to hide the severity of her illness from me because she did not want me to drop out of school. Nana came to New York to stay with my mother while I returned to campus.

In May of 1985, Mary lost her battle with cancer. I was on campus trying to complete my spring semester. My mother made sacrifices for me to finish college and have an adventurous life. Before she passed, I remember asking why she separated from my father and whether I could trust him. She explained that she stayed with him to ensure I received the best life and had options and opportunities to succeed. Once I was accepted into college, she contacted TWA, my father's employer for over 20 years, to inquire about educational benefits, which would have paid for my college tuition. She discovered those benefits were being used by "his daughter for nursing school." I was Duke's only daughter. My mother was angry and embarrassed.

She confided that the nights my father was away from home, he was not playing cards with a friend but having an affair with the woman upstairs. Instead of educating me, my father listed this woman as his daughter so she could earn her nursing degree. My mother was infuriated and decided there was no longer any reason to stay with my father, which is why she moved out of their apartment during my freshman year of college. If she knew my father was having an affair, why did she remain in the marriage? Was this the role of motherhood, sacrifices? Why would she trade her happiness for mine? I always knew my mother loved me, but this was more than I could fathom. All my life and through random conversations, she would say, "Sit up straight, eat your vegetables, keep the bathroom clean, and never live with a man." She made me promise I would never live with a man and that I should live by myself for one year before I decided to marry anyone.

I wish my mother had shared the details of her health with me. I would have been there caring for her. Instead, she died in her sleep in the hospital room. About 1 a.m., Momma Doe called me from Boston and told me my mother had died. I felt numb and alone. My mother, who gave me life and unconditional love, was gone. I loved my mother and prayed that I would make her proud of me and honor all the promises I made. Wondering if God would transfer some of Mary's spirit to me, I looked around our apartment confused and angry. What was I supposed to do now? I rolled over and cried myself to sleep. Thank God for Aunt Eleanor and Nana; they handled all the burial plans and scheduled her service to happen in Boston.

Mary wanted to be cremated and have her ashes sprinkled in the ocean in Boston so she could continue to travel. After the service, I sprinkled her ashes in the Boston Bay. The following day, I remember walking into Momma Doe's kitchen where people were wishing everyone a Happy Mother's Day. I was so overwhelmed with grief I had not noticed it was Mother's Day. My family was honoring their mothers while I mourned mine. Tears began falling and I felt alone.

Before leaving Boston, while riding in the car with Charlene and other cousins talking about marriages and life, I commented about my parents' marriage. Charlene quickly corrected me. She told me that my parents were not married.

"Your mother did not want you to know, but you should know the truth," Charlene said.

Still grieving my mother's death, I raised my voice and almost jumped out of the car.

"No one ever told me this before. You are lying," I replied.

Shaking her head while driving, she continued, "You should know the truth."

The ride back to the house seemed like an eternity. Running into Nana's room, I immediately phoned Aunt Eleanor for the truth. Picking up the phone, I could hear her taking a deep breath and ask, "Who told you that?" After I retold the story of the car ride, she confirmed the information.

"Your mother didn't want you to know; she asked us to honor her secret," Aunt Eleanor said.

Nana came into the room during the call and overheard the conversation. When the call ended, she responded, "I am sorry you found out like this, but your mother asked us not to tell you."

Sitting on the edge of Nana's bed, I was confused; my mind began racing back to our mother and daughter conversations and her stern admonitions: "Eat your vegetables. Sit up straight and never live with a man." It now made sense. Nana reminded me of the love and sacrifices mothers make for their children.

"It's something that you will never understand until you become a mother. Your mother loved you and your birth changed her life," Nana explained. "Everything was about you having the best she could offer. Do not judge her; she loved you. Hurry up and finish school and make her proud."

When I returned to Howard the next day, I marched into my dean's office and changed my major from Nutrition & Dietetics to

Food and Nutrition. I met all of the science requirements for this new major, did not have to take Organic Chemistry, and now I could concentrate on culinary and management courses. My mother was gone and remaining in that major was a huge burden to carry. Once the dean approved the switch, I was assigned a new adviser and an enormous weight was lifted off my shoulders. No more organic chemistry classes in Death Valley.

Eventually, I emptied the apartment in New York and moved all the furniture to D.C., where I found an apartment with my classmate Jodi. We furnished the entire apartment with everything from my mother's home. Being an only child, I inherited everything. Instead of buying furniture, we were able to put a month's rent in reserve. I was now responsible for making my own home and starting new memories. I always kept a clean kitchen and bathroom. My mother taught me well; and I paid my bills on time like Momma Doe taught me—especially my car insurance. The weekend we moved in, I went to a party and met a man named Randy Berry, a member of the Alpha Phi Alpha fraternity, who recently moved into my complex. Randy taught me how to play chess and introduced me to sushi. This was the beginning of a great year.

During the summer of 1985, I received a call from the woman who had hired me as a nanny. She asked if I could be the children's nanny for the summer. They were planning a trip to the South of France, London, and Paris. My expenses would be paid in addition to a $650 weekly salary. After accepting the job offer, I learned my employer neglected to mention I would be staying alone with the children in a villa in France for two weeks. However, she arranged for us to have a cook, and I had one day off a week. I understood how Nana felt on her days off—freedom. Although we dined at the finest restaurants and traveled first class throughout Europe, I learned that finishing college was important. Being a nanny to wealthy families did not interest me, regardless of how much money I made. My freedom and independence were more important to me in my twenties. My mother made life sacrifices for me to be happy and have options. Well, I would not disappoint her dreams.

Before leaving Paris, I made a long-distance phone call to Aunt Eleanor, asking her if I could stay in Paris for a year and then return to complete school. She refused my request. Then, I called JoAnn.

"Hey sis, I'm in Paris and want to know if I could take a year off from school."

JoAnn's response was, "Ask Roger, your brother-in-law."

"No," Roger said.

Both families denied my request and said to come home, telling me I would be free to return to Paris once I graduated from Howard University, and only then. Unbeknownst to me, my mother asked all of them to watch over me in the event she died before I completed school. I was unaware of the promise they made to my mother to make sure I completed college. Afraid to disobey my family and just stay in Paris, I returned and completed my final year.

In the fall of 1985, I would be a senior in college. Nana called and said, "Hurry up!" and "Are you planning on graduating this year? I am not getting any younger."

The school year began, and I was elated about my new classes. My favorite classes were Culinary 101 and 102. We managed the cafeteria on the lower floor of the Human Ecology Building. There were seven students in the class, and we had rotating positions. As cafeteria managers, we created the menu, modified the recipes and handled all the shopping. Jodi and I were classmates and roommates, which was a perk for completing class assignments. We assigned each other to our favorite positions; mine was baker and manager, and Jodi enjoyed preparing the salads and being the head chef. The class required us to prepare a full-course lunch, soup or salad, cold sandwich, hot meal, fresh breads and desserts, and homemade cold beverage every Wednesday. By the time noon arrived, the students and staff were lined up and down the hall waiting to eat a homemade meal for only $4. It was exciting and rewarding. I was convinced this was the correct career choice.

As a senior, we had to complete an externship. My choice was the hotel/restaurant assignment. It sounded exciting. However, in reality, the hours were long, and the weekends were grueling. Also, during my training, the manager responsible for my rotation made unwanted sexual advances. Unaware of how to handle his comments, I smiled and pretended that I didn't hear him, hoping he would get the hint and stop. During our weekly meeting, he reminded me that as my manager, his grade and comments would determine whether I passed or failed the externship. I scheduled a meeting with my adviser and shared a "What if" problem. I had not previously encountered sexual harassment and was scared about reporting his behavior. However, the sexual comments and invitations kept escalating. My adviser explained that it was not uncommon for men to make sexual advances toward women, especially young students. This type of harassment would continue throughout a woman's career, she said, and it was important for women not to doubt their character or let any man scar them for life. My adviser asked if I needed to report a real problem or was someone in trouble?

"No!" I replied and stood up to leave her office.

"Odell, you are smarter than this problem, and I am here if you need to talk," she said as I walked to the door. She gave me her home telephone number.

When I returned to the externship assignment, my manager told me I needed to complete the closing shift rotation. He reserved a room in the hotel for me to stay that night instead of driving home at midnight. Smiling, he looked confident that I would comply with his sexual advances. I dropped my head and walked towards the door, feeling defeated.

Before opening the office door, I said, "I remember a previous conversation where you mentioned having a heart attack two years ago. How will I know the difference between your climax and another heart attack?"

He opened his eyes wide as if he saw a ghost. Before my shift ended, he told me I did not have to work the closing shift and was free to leave early. The following week, my adviser informed me she had received all the required paperwork and that I passed my externship. We never discussed this topic again.

I graduated on the Dean's List in Food and Nutrition. My friends

Angel, Robin, Sarah and Alonzo, and Nana, attended graduation. Charlene, JoAnn and Roger had car trouble and never made it but they called me to say congratulations. Nana was so proud of my accomplishment, she kept saying, "It took you long enough." When I changed my major to Nutrition and Dietetics, it added another year to my studies, but it was worth it. My cousin Darsweil, his father, my brothers, and my nephew Monty drove up from Virginia. Aunt Eleanor and Uncle Lyle gave me my first VCR as a graduation present, saying, "Record your TV shows and don't just come home from work, get involved." No matter how much love and happiness I felt, the absence of both my mothers was noticeable. I was off to a new chapter in my life; I learned to accept the love and support from those present.

A month before graduation, I had accepted a position in the minority supervisor program at the Willard Straight Hall Dining Program of Cornell University. Leaving D.C. and heading to Ithaca, New York, was challenging, but looking forward to my first full-time job was rewarding. I ended the weekend with a graduation party and hanging with my friends. Before leaving DC, Randy gave me this poem.

ONE IN TWO HALVES
Two images clashing and colliding yet
Side by side they walk.
A crescendo of Personality, Bourgeois Intellect
an expression of city thought.
The lady is a mirror.
A reflection of two of her-selves
Like light and darkness emanating from their wells
Strength is the shield of her soul it seems.
Prepared to endure the battles that await her.
Nothing shall conquer her dreams.
Onward charges Odell slashing through life's fallacies.
Realizing that through truth, she will defeat
All of Life's Bitter tragedy

CHAPTER 3

INTERRUPTION: YOU PROMISED ME!

CORNELL UNIVERSITY

I PACKED UP THE CHEVY AND drove to Ithaca, New York, headed towards a new chapter in my life. Cornell University's hiring package included relocation costs and two weeks of temporary housing, allowing me time to secure my first solo apartment. The drive from D.C. to Ithaca was exciting and emotional. I was leaving close friends, a culture and community that represented my values and heritage to embark on a new life in upstate New York. The summer day was bright, and the sun was shining on my face. I could feel the warm breeze coming through the windows. The radio played 107.5 WBLS-FM, and I was bobbing my head to the music. As the music played, I was moving further away from my past and closer to my destiny.

Driving through the small, rural towns, I reflected on the conversation with my adviser when she approved the transfer to her department. We talked about my dreams and discussed various career paths in the field of Food and Nutrition. She shared a brochure from the Cornell University Dining Minority Supervisor Training Program and encouraged me to stay focused and open to this career opportunity. I still hear her words echoing in my head as if it was yesterday: "You are young, talented, and an honor student. Once you graduate from Howard University with Cornell Dining on your resume, you will be an asset to any company. You will have your choice of career options." If accepted into the Cornell Dining Program, my adviser suggested that I stay a minimum of four years to learn everything they offered. I left her office motivated and committed to the challenge. Three months before graduation, Cornell Dining offered me a job beginning at the end of June 1986. I was excited! Nana said, "Your mother would be proud." She promised to visit me before the winter set in.

It was high noon when I pulled into the parking lot of Cornell University's Willard Straight Dining Hall, or "the Straight" as it was called, ready to begin my new job. My program director Stu had instructed me to park in the back of the building, where he would meet me inside and direct me to the hotel. As I proudly walked through the building, I noticed a few White students staring at me. Immediately, my defenses went on high alert. The student population looked completely different from what I was used to at Howard University. Glancing down at my clothes to make sure they weren't falling off, I realized I was wearing my red shirt, which read, "Black by Popular Demand. Howard University." Not feeling intimidated by their stares, my head went up. I threw my shoulders back and began walking with more pride. When I arrived at the dining hall, a short white male dressed in shirt and tie approached me with a smile. The first words out of his mouth were, "I hope you brought me a shirt. I like it!" Lowering my defenses, I smiled and again felt comfortable about my decision to accept this new job.

Once settled in my apartment, I began browsing around town to familiarize myself with my new community. I discovered that the town had one movie theater, and it played the movie *La Bamba* all summer long. While driving through the campus, a student asked if I was lost, pointing me towards North Campus. Later, I learned that most socially, politically conscious students lived on the North Campus in the Ujamaa ("cooperative economics") dormitory.

Monday morning, I arrived at work ready and eager to begin my training. I was the youngest supervisor in the entire dining department. Most of my coworkers were married or living with a significant

other. Most of the kitchen staff were Black, and the servers were older White women who had worked the food stations for years. Cornell University was the primary employer for the community. My
goal was to keep a low profile and stay observant. Howard University Management 101 taught me not to socialize with people under
my supervision, remain neutral. The Black employees were trying to
discern if they could trust me. A few weeks into training, a White
female student supervisor began inviting me to socialize with her on
the weekends at Dunbar's, a local bar, but I wasn't a beer drinker, so
my social life looked bleak.

At first glance, Ithaca did not appear to have a strong community
of young Black professionals. Therefore, whenever I had a weekend
off, I spent my money on a round-trip plane ticket to Washington,
D.C., reconnecting with my cousin and roommate and hoping to
find Randy. During any given weekend in D.C., I watched every new
movie, waited in line to eat at the Florida Avenue Grill, and danced
to the Go-Go Funk of Chuck Brown. I purchased all the latest jazz,
R&B, and hip-hop albums for my growing eclectic musical collection. Sunday night, I flew back to Ithaca. On Monday morning, I
chanted to myself, "Stay four years. With Cornell and Howard on
your resume, you will be in charge of your future."

After my first winter in Ithaca, my trips to D.C. were limited.
Looking out the window at all the snow, I could not believe the
schools were still open. Washington, D.C. would have closed the city
based on the snow on top of my car. I adjusted my plans to stay a
minimum of two years.

One morning shortly after starting my new job, I arrived at work
greeted by my coworkers, who appeared to be laughing at me, the new
supervisor from D.C. It must have been initiation day because they
had jokes at my expense all day. One of my coworkers was a Black
man named Michael. We were the only Black supervisors in our unit.
Finally, during lunch that day, Michael and the other supervisors told
me why they were laughing. It had to do with how I was selected for

the position. They started laughing again. Stu overheard the noise and came waltzing into the office to share his side of the story.

Stu recalled that day when the men were in Stu's office reviewing applications for the position but mainly looking for a male who played basketball to join their intramural team. My resume caught Michael's attention.

"Look, here's a good candidate, Odell," Michael said. "This candidate is a man because my uncle's name is Odell. This resume says he likes chess and basketball and is attending Howard University. He's perfect."

Stu had human resources arrange an interview, which explained why they all seemed shocked and confused on the day I arrived for the interview.

"Nonetheless," Stu said, "I hired you because you were good."

Michael was tired of me complaining about the lack of social options in Ithaca, so he invited me to a spot where he bragged about the DJ. It was not the same as D.C., and the DJ only played three Black artists, Janet Jackson's song "Control," Michael Jackson's "Bad," and Timex Social Club's "Rumors." And everyone danced to Steve Winwood's "Higher Love." Whenever the DJ played these songs in the rotation, Michael and I danced as if our lives depended on it. It became our weekly night out. In the spring, we began touring the Finger Lakes winery, chilling in the park, and enjoying occasional drinks after work. Soon the other coworkers joined us for happy hours. It was not uncommon for me to see men drunk on the weekends and functional on Monday morning. Michael and I began spending more time together, and my trips to D.C. were less frequent. We enjoyed playing chess and cooking together. He was tall and had a deep voice like my father; he was creative and meticulous in the kitchen. If my mother were alive, she would have loved him and been proud to work with him on catering events. When Nana came to visit, I arranged a poker game with my coworkers. It surprised them that an 80-year-old woman beat them at poker. Because we started dating, Michael was moved into another dining hall to avoid any relational conflict, which was good because I was committed to learning and growing professionally within my new reduced timeframe.

Cornell Dining offered some of the best culinary experiences. They were famous for their Cross-Country Dinners where they selected a 5-star restaurant from the United States to replicate their décor and menu in every dining unit. The meals were always a success and a new culinary phenomenon. My first experience left me spellbound. However, before another round of Cross-Country Dinners, I approached Stu and asked if we could host a Black History Dinner in February. My coworkers examined the pros and cons and discussed a menu. Stu echoed the concerns from the other directors that, traditionally, all the units had low attendance on Friday nights. Promising the team we would have a positive turnout, I quickly contacted the residence hall director at Ujamaa and asked for his assistance in spreading the word. Those were the students who missed their mommas' cooking.

Everyone was committed to supporting the first Black History Dinner at Cornell Dining. This dinner would be Willard Straight Dining Hall's first annual Black History Dinner or its last. The chef immediately began asking the other Black cooks experienced with southern foods to work that night. We had to train the White cooks on preparing fresh collard greens, candied yams, dirty rice, seasoned fried chicken, and baked macaroni and cheese not cooked with cheese sauce. Cooks argued about shredding all the cheese. They did not know the difference between a cheese sauce and using shredded cheese. The bakery made sweet potato and apple pies, cornbread, and bread pudding.

Stu allowed me to offer a special soul food dish every day leading up to the big event to entice the students to return and dine at the Straight on Friday night. He also approved placing educational tent cards on the dining tables. I designed cards about George Washington Carver, Langston Hughes, Mary McCleod Bethune, W.E.B DuBois, Frederick Douglass, Dr. Charles Drew, and others. I noticed the students were not reading them. Therefore, I created a challenge. If a student could locate a typo or error on the cards (which didn't exist), they would be allowed to drink extra beverages during late-night meals; this usually wasn't allowed. Before you knew it, all students of all races were reading the tent cards and being educated about Black

History. Because the student supervisors were required to know the menu and the ingredients of the foods listed on the menu, one of the student supervisors created a cheat sheet that said, "How to Survive Black History Month with Odell." She and I eventually became good friends. I never had the chance to tell Denise that she was the first White girl I ever called a friend.

Friday night arrived, and I could sense the staff was nervous. When we opened the doors for dinner, the line extended outside the door and up the stairs. The same grateful feelings I had when we opened the cafeteria for lunch at Howard returned. The students and staff of all cultural backgrounds had come to Willard Straight for the Black History Dinner.

The dining hall filled up quickly. The chef from the North Campus called and congratulated us. The other units had low turnout, and they were able to come and support the Straight. I was delighted and thankful for the support. I stood in the center of the dining hall smiling and reflecting on all the family dinners I had growing up in Boston, with family coming by dropping off their favorite dishes for dinner. It was great! Stu was all smiles and asked me, "What's next?"

Next was an African Dinner in the fall of 1987. We again informed the Ujamaa dormitory about the upcoming dinner. Willard Straight staff and student supervisors converted the Ivy Dining Room into a room with an African motif (decorations, cardboard animals, and music).

The menu was authentic, and the attendance and support again exceeded our expectations. Many Black professionals from the community, whom I had not seen before, dined at the Straight. WE DID IT!! The Ujamaa residential director submitted an article about the impact of the first Black History Dinners on campus. They honored me with a Thank You plaque that still hangs in my home office today.

Michael and I were still dating; however, he did not understand why I could not move in with him. My mother made me promise never to live with a man and to live alone for one year before getting married. I could hear my mother's voice ringing in my head, "Sit up straight, eat your vegetables, keep the bathroom clean, and never live with a man." I intended to keep this latter promise to my mother, and I did, until November 1987 when Michael and I were married in New Haven, Connecticut, during Thanksgiving weekend.

The 1988 spring semester was winding down. After the African Dinner, I noticed that professors and professionals from the community began coming into Straight Dining Hall more often and introducing themselves to me. One professor asked me if I had pledged a sorority while attending Howard. Unfortunately, I had not due to being a transfer student, then carrying extra credits, and losing my mother the year I could attend a rush. She took my contact information and promised to be in touch. Here I was living in Ithaca, a predominately White collegiate community, with the opportunity to pledge a Black sorority. Remarkable! In the spring of 1988, the Delta Sigma Theta Sorority, Inc. invited me to their Ithaca Alumni Chapter Rush. There were six of us who were accepted to the spring line.

Lined up in formation based on our height, I was second in line. A woman named Joy was first in line. While we were pledging, as part of the sorority enrollment process, Joy drove from New Jersey every weekend to Ithaca and stayed at my house. We were both newlyweds and the same age, which allowed us to bond beyond our sorority interests. The other line sisters were older and married with children. As part of our initiation into the Deltas, we had to read a series of statements. I was nervous and began to stutter. My heart raced, and I was mortified. That I was a Howard University graduate unable to speak with confidence was terrifying. I overheard the sorority sisters talking about extending our meeting time or starting earlier to accommodate my stuttering. It was then that I promised myself and them I would not stutter during any future events. Once we completed the pledging process and were officially inducted into the sorority, my big sisters gave me the name "Persistent," which described my behavior during the pledge process.

CHAPTER 4

INTERRUPTION: GOD-FAMILY-CAREER

I HOPED THAT MICHAEL WOULD CHANGE his mind about advancing our careers and leaving Ithaca once he learned how valuable his skills were in the world. Without his permission, I submitted his resume to Marriott Corporation. Their salary and benefits package was remarkable, and when offered, Michael agreed to accept the position and leave Ithaca.

My adviser was right about the opportunities that awaited me. In June of 1988, I resigned from Cornell University and accepted a manager's position with Marriott at Yale-New Haven Hospital in the Healthcare Division. I was 26 years old and had Howard University, Cornell Dining, and now Marriott /Yale Hospital on my resume. Michael was offered a position with Marriott in the Education Division working at the University of Bridgeport. Our game plan was to stay three to four years in these new positions in Connecticut and then move south.

Although I never had the opportunity to say goodbye to my sorority sisters before leaving Ithaca, I was excited about our new life. My professional career was promising, and I was now working in food and nutrition, where I was thriving. The move was also significant because I knew that if Michael and I were going to start a family, I needed to live near my family—most of whom lived in New Haven—who had experience raising children. I was in college when they had their children. JoAnn and Roger now had four children, and Charlene had two daughters, the oldest of which was the flower girl at my wedding.

Life was good. We were newlyweds and spending time with the

married couples in my family. We occasionally spent our weekends partying at local clubs with real soul and rhythm and blues music. It was great to be home. Two years after moving to New Haven, I gave birth to our daughter, Jacqueline Diane Cooper. My friend Tony from Pratt kept his promise and became Jackie's godfather, along with Stu and Angel. I wanted Jackie to have a range of support. Two years later, our son Jonathan Michael Cooper was born, and Jodi, Brenda, who I met working at Yale, and my director from Yale/Marriott, Melissa Zelazny, became his godparents. People were surprised because they were White, but I wanted my children to have cultural options. Melissa was down to earth and her husband, Zee, enjoyed hunting. I felt their love for the outdoors would appeal to Jonathan and provide him with options in life that did not exist in the urban community. JoAnn's youngest daughter, Tanya, was 16 years old and also became godmother to both Jackie and Jonathan. If anything happened to my husband and me, the kids would remain with family.

I kept in touch with my brothers in Virginia, and we occasionally drove down for long weekends as a family. Ben had married and had another son around Jackie's age. We visited for years before Ben and Montez's mother took ill and passed of cancer. Returning for the funeral, I felt sad; she treated me like a daughter. When I read her obituary, it said, "mother to two sons, Ben and Montez, and daughter Odell." I was shocked and honored. When we returned home, I checked in with Nana, which led to a new reality for both of us.

CARING FOR THE CAREGIVER

Nana was 95 years old and still living in Boston with Momma Doe, who was selling her house and planning to move to Connecticut. I moved Nana to my home in Connecticut. My husband reluctantly agreed to the transition, but I was adamant about caring for her. It was my turn. My children would have the same opportunity to experience the undeniable love of their great-grandmother that I had. Nana loved being a great-grandmother and enjoyed spending time with the kids. She began teaching Jonathan how to play poker while teaching Jackie to embrace the love of baseball. After Nana moved in, it became more difficult to hide the problems in my marriage. I guess this is why Michael didn't want her to move in. As a married woman, I was taught to remain silent about my marital problems, deal with them, keep praying, and it will eventually get better. One of the problems was Michael's drinking. I quickly learned that there is a difference between being a social drinker and alcoholism.

GOD IS CALLING

I started attending church as an outlet and prayed for God to resolve the issues in my marriage. Attending the mega multi-cultural church in West Haven with my family, I continued to keep up the persona that everything was OK in my marriage.

The church had a strong and effective youth ministry, and the pastor was an excellent teacher of the gospel. While attending, I learned more about the Christian bible and accepted Christ as my Lord and Savior, placing my personal faith and trust in Him. In the Christian faith, we believe no one is saved by the faith of others. No one is forgiven by doing certain deeds. The only way to be saved is to personally accept Jesus as your Savior.

"If you declare with your mouth, 'Jesus is Lord,' and believe in your heart that God raised him from the dead, you are saved," according to Romans 10:9 of the Bible.

Even though my faith was growing, my marriage was rapidly declining. Michael tried to attend church but suggested we join a Black church. He missed singing the traditional cultural gospel songs, and he was committed to saving our marriage.

Around this time, my coworker invited our family to attend an historical Black church.

"You should stop using your gifts for other people and use them for God," she said. "We have a young pastor at our church, and I think you would enjoy worshipping there."

One Sunday, the family visited and joined Varick African Methodist Episcopal Zion Church in New Haven, under the leadership of Rev. McCorn. After we joined the church, I became more involved in the ministry, and my pastor began developing my spiritual gifts. The children and my husband joined the choir. Jackie always walked her brother downstairs to his Sunday school class for the youth. There he met Marcel Brown and they began what would become a lifelong friendship.

Attending a Black church did not save or change the issues in my marriage. Ultimately, I decided to move out of our three-level, modern furnished apartment with two kids and a 97-year-old grandmother. All I could afford was a two-bedroom apartment, and I opted to sleep on the couch. I did not want my children to experience the same discomforts as I did by sleeping on the couch. I was determined to break the family cycle. Michael eventually relocated to Atlanta and enrolled in a Christian-based program for men with addictions.

While we were separated, I began teaching Christian education classes and assisted the pastor in training and developing lay leaders. My first workshop was called "Spiritual Gifts." The disciples—developing lay leaders –would complete a written questionnaire and attend a 12-hour workshop to identify their spiritual gifts. This assessment was used to guide disciples into various platforms of ministry. Rev. McCorn was interested in community organizing and building relationships with ECCO (Elm City Community Organization), which had a mission to partner with faith-based organizations to address issues in the urban community and seek resolutions for improvement. The organization began challenging slum landlords and redlining, the systematic denial of services, either by explicitly or selectively raising prices to residents of specific neighborhoods or communities, often based on race. I was responsible for coordinating lay leaders in the church to attend the local ECCO training sessions with the lead organizer. Pastor eventually elevated my role and created a new ministry. I was now Minister Odell Montgomery Cooper of the Training and Lay Involvement Ministry. According to Ephesian 4:11 of the Christian bible: "Now these are the gifts Christ gave to the church, the apostles, the prophets, the evangelists, the pastors, and teachers, to equip his people for works of service, so that the body of Christ may be built up."

I noticed that my stuttering had disappeared. I remember reading in the bible that anyone who is in Christ is a new creation. The old Odell was gone; the new creation was here! I began walking and talking through my new life. Pastor McCorn allowed us to be an innovative ministry.

One day Rev. McCorn recommended I attend the Black Ministries Program (BMP) at Hartford Seminary. The Pastor respected the program for new ministers seeking to grow stronger in their faith and understanding of the bible. He said this program would be valuable and answer all my questions about God and my faith. Originally, I only registered to take the Old and New Testament class to become a better Sunday school teacher. The seminary program convened every Saturday from 9 a.m. to noon for one academic year. Therefore, I needed a sitter for my children. Fortunately, Charlene lived nearby, and her oldest daughter was 16 years old. She volunteered to watch my kids every weekend with my Nana. This behavior was remarkable: What 16-year-old teenager would sacrifice Friday nights and Saturday afternoons for one year?

The BMP was an awesome experience! The class structure resembled that of Howard University. Hartford Seminary's Black Ministries Program is a national model for building laity and clergy leadership, training, and preaching skills in the urban church. The BMP director was Rev. Dr. Judy Fentress Williams and featured an exceptional staff of Black biblical scholars, who related the scriptures through the lens of the Black experience. I was naïve in understanding the biblical scriptures at the time I enrolled. However, these professors were world-renowned biblical scholars, teaching in a certificate program in Hartford. I connected with great people who were on track to become ministers and pastors in their denominations. My calling, I was convinced, was to be the best Sunday school teacher I could become. In the program, I befriended another student, Brenda Lammie, who lived in Hartford. When my two classes were over, Brenda convinced me to complete the entire program, and I agreed. We studied on weekends and took every class together, except for preaching.

Months before I completed BMP, Michael unexpectedly returned to Connecticut from Atlanta. He said God told him to come home.

Every night, I would pray in my corner for him to leave. I overheard his prayers for God to change my mind about our marriage. Every morning, I would wake up and verbalize my anger and discontent to him about his return. I was adamant about him leaving. Three days after his arrival, I woke up and sat on the edge of Nana's bed and began scanning my soul for the anger and belittling words to pierce his heart again. I squeezed my eyes and began spiraling through my body, scanning every inch for the hate. When I came up empty, I scanned again and again. Something must have been wrong; where was the hate? I needed it. It was then I realized God was directing me because I no longer hated him, and I was no longer angry about our past. Then I surrendered. I sat there in disbelief and knew only God could have removed my disdain and hate for his presence. Moments later, I found Michael sitting at the kitchen table waiting for the hateful words to spew out of my mouth, but there were none. They were gone.

My friends thought I had lost my mind and could not understand how I could hate him the night before on our phone calls, yet the same hate and the pain that accompanied it were gone the next morning. Some of them did not believe me, but I think because this all involved my husband, they accepted it. Some friends faded into the background and stopped calling me because they could not believe I was going back into this relationship, doing this again.

I shared my morning experience with my husband, and he began crying. Later that month, we renewed our wedding vows on the same weekend I was scheduled to graduate from Hartford Seminary.

I graduated from the seminary's BMP program in June 1997. Attending the ceremony on Friday were Aunt Eleanor and Uncle Lyle, who drove up from Brooklyn, Jodi, my children, my niece Doe, and Rev. McCorn. Michael could not take the day off from work to attend the ceremony because he was taking the next day off for our vow renewal.

Saturday afternoon, Michael and I renewed our wedding vows in a church member's backyard. Rev. McCorn officiated, our children participated in the ceremony, and this time everyone was present. Angel organized the wedding coordinator, my cousin Kim was my matron of honor, my brother Ben gave me away. This role helped ease his disappointment that he and my brother Montez missed the original wedding because of inclement weather. Darsweil drove up from New York. Jonathan Berryman, who was the choir director at our church, stood with my husband. This ceremony was what Michael and I needed to begin anew.

We purchased our first home a year later in the Westville community of New Haven, and I was baptized at Christian Tabernacle Church in Hamden. Our entire family was active in the life of the church, and the house and marriage were good. My coworker, who invited me to Varick Church, became my spiritual godmother.

God was using my gifts in ministry. Witnessing the blessings on my life and desire to learn more about God and my faith, Rev. McCorn began assigning books for me to read and report on what I learned. One of the books was Upon This Rock: The Miracles of a Black Church. He mentioned that his fraternity brother was in the book, but Rev. McCorn was reassigned to a church in Chicago before I could finish the book. In my selfish anger, I stopped reading the book. The new pastor and I had a difference of theological opinion and after a year I decided to leave the church. Consulting the family, we agreed to transfer our membership to Bethel AME Church in Bloomfield, which was 45 minutes north of my house. Bethel's pastor was Rev. Dr. Alvan Johnson, one of my professors in the BMP, and Rev. Brenda Lammie and her family attended. After taking Dr. Johnson's Black Liberation Theology class and reading the book Upon This Rock, I wanted to learn more about Black Liberation Theology. I was blessed to experience the teaching and witnessed how to infuse the living word of Black Liberation Theology into ministry. Brenda's family became an extension of mine. Brenda had three sons. The youngest and my son, Jonathan, became inseparable. The family traveled to Bloomfield twice a week for service, bible study, and other weekend activities for the next ten years. Our families started a new tradition and began spending New Year's Eve together. On New Year's Day, we would cook a traditional New Year's Day meal of black-eyed peas and rice, fried chicken, and macaroni and cheese. After dinner, we played Scrabble.

Michael began coordinating plans for us to travel to New York to spend time with his side of the family. He had two sisters living in New York with their children. Jackie and Jonathan loved visiting their aunt because she made the best macaroni and cheese.

SPIRITUAL REVELATION

One Friday, while in Hartford, Brenda asked if I would accompany her to Hartford Seminary. She was attending the master's degree program orientation. I agreed to go rather than drive back to New Haven. It was a beautiful sunny day, and while she was listening to the dean, I quietly sat in the corner of the room. Before leaving the orientation, my information was on the enrollment application for the fall.

Classes began in two months, and I had to explain to my husband that I was enrolled in the master's program part-time in Hartford and would continue working on my career while being a mother, a caretaker for Nana, and a wife. He could sense the passion in my eyes, and by now, Michael knew that once I believed in a purpose, trying to change my mind was a futile discussion.

Ultimately, I had to place Nana, who was now 100 years old, in a nursing home to make sure she received the best care. I was working for a small computer company in a position requiring that I travel, and I was also attending seminary school twice a week.

While we drove to Bloomfield one Sunday morning, nine-year-old Jackie turned around in her car seat and, sounding like a grown brimstone pastor, harshly reprimanded her brother.

"Jonathan, you are going to hell. God will not let you play with your Gameboy in heaven unless you give your life to Christ. Mommy, Dad, and I are going to heaven, and you won't be there!"

She then began paraphrasing a lesson she learned in Sunday school.

"For God so loved the world that he gave his one and only Son, that whoever believes in him shall not perish but have eternal life," she said, reciting the scripture John 3:16.

Later, during the church service, Rev. Johnson invited anyone who wanted to join the church or accept Christ as their Lord and Savior to come to the altar. Jonathan bolted out of the seat and ran down the aisle toward the pulpit. I tried to catch him, thinking he was confused about the offer. Rev. Johnson and the congregation began laughing at this young child who ran to the altar like an adult in need of the redemptive blood of Christ. Pastor Johnson asked Jonathan why he was coming to the altar.

"I want to go to heaven!" Jonathan replied.

Although Jackie had already given her life to Christ, she would not let her brother stand alone. She asked Pastor Johnson if he could baptize them together. Both Jackie and Jonathan attended baptism class and were baptized the following month. Brenda and her husband stood in as their spiritual godparents.

GOOD-BYE DADDY DUKE

During my first year in seminary school, I received a call from a woman in New York who introduced herself as my father's medical caretaker, telling me he was in the hospital. I recognized her name from a conversation with my mother. She was the woman my father listed as his daughter, allowing her to receive my educational benefits.

The woman found my father on the floor in his apartment and took him to the hospital. The caller was the woman who had disrespected my mother and had stolen my educational benefits. I did not know if I should thank her or curse her. Years ago, I admitted my father into a nursing home so he could receive better and consistent medical care. However, he checked himself out of the center and arranged for this woman to provide his care. Hearing her voice sent chills up my spine. She gave me the details of his location. I said thank you and hung up. Later that evening, I phoned my brothers and promised I would keep them updated on his condition. I did not have a sense of urgency to drive to New York. When I arrived three days later, I found out that my father had transitioned in his sleep on March 17, 1998—St. Patrick's Day. I phoned my brothers in Virginia, and we discussed how to handle his remains. We agreed that our father should be cremated, none of us wanting to organize a viewing. I had never met any of my father's friends and had no idea how to reach them. He did not have an insurance policy, and we agreed to split the cremation cost three ways. My brothers did not want his belongings, except for the oil painting hanging on the closet door. My husband and three of my cousins drove from New Haven to Manhattan to empty his apartment.

I looked around the apartment, and it seemed unloved and desolate. Although it resembled my home, it felt stale. On all the visits I made home, we barely spoke or spent father and daughter time alone. My mother was always in the room, ear hustling our small talk. My father sat in his leather recliner in the bedroom watching TV or eating a home-cooked meal my mother would make every day. He never picked me up from the bus station or dropped me off. My mother always took a cab. I rode in his brown Lincoln Continental once when my mother made him drive us through Times Square to see the Christmas lights. I sat in the back seat, too afraid to move or speak. Every Christmas and birthday card I received from my parents was signed "Love Mommy and Daddy"– always in the same handwriting. I later recognized my mother's signature and determined that she signed the cards. My father never met my husband and had only seen Jackie when she was a year old.

I stared at the picture of the woman in the gold frame that sat on the table behind my father's chair. It was signed "To Duke. Thank you for the memories, Marilyn." I guess I would never know who Marilyn was to my father now that he had passed. I asked my brother-in-law Roger whether he thought I should contact this woman and tell her about my father's passing. He picked up the picture and began laughing, showing it to the other men in the house.

"No, that won't be necessary," they all replied in unison.

I responded with an attitude, "That picture, autographed to my father, sat on that table for most of my life."

They continued to laugh until tears rolled down their faces. Roger stumbled over to the stack of porn magazines and selected one with the woman in the magazine. It was entitled, Interview with Porn Star, Marilyn Chambers.

A daughter should not ever be responsible for discarding her father's private belongings. Roger and the others departed the apartment with plenty of magazines. I did not know anyone in my father's family; he never spoke about them. All we knew was that my father was born in Savannah, Georgia. He lived with and was raised by Leila and Garfield Philpott.

I found a document stating that Duke B. Montgomery was honorably discharged from the Merchant Marines. My father earned a Ph.D. from the streets of Harlem. He was a numbers runner and heavily immersed in the Harlem nightlife during the '50s and '60s. Amazingly, Duke never engaged in drugs and did not drink alcohol.

My brothers and I are convinced that we have additional siblings somewhere in this world. My father was not an overly loving man, but he provided the only way he knew how. Duke was one generation away from being a slave and lived at a time when sharecropping was the main livelihood for Blacks in the south and during the Great Migration north. He was persistent and a survivor. He could have been hung, incarcerated, or killed. Thanks to God, none of these things happened to him. He was a survivor.

Our mothers obviously found something captivating about our father as they had children with him. Regardless, Duke B. Montgomery was a veteran and deserved a proper burial. My brother Montez wanted us to come to Virginia and give our father a memorial and pray over his remains. I declined the offer and permitted him to move forward with his plans. Montez arranged for him to be buried in Suffolk, Virginia, Veterans Cemetery.

We packed up the items we wanted. I wrapped the oil painting in a big blanket and walked down two flights of stairs.

CHAPTER 5

INTERRUPTION: A TIME WHEN
I HAD DIFFERENT DREAMS

THE COOPER HOUSEHOLD WAS DOING WELL. We were a typical, happy, middle-class family with two children and caring for Nana in the nursing home, which she enjoyed. Michael and I were raising our children and nurturing them through school. Jackie excelled in every grade, and Jonathan was the quiet, average student. We continued to worship at Bethel Bloomfield, enjoying the couples' life with the Lammies . . . until Jonathan's birthday when our neighbor came over with a bottle of Kahlua and everyone had a drink.

The next day, the tides began to shift. Michael had been sober for seven years, and then the drinking and marital problems returned. Like an overflowing toilet, they just kept coming and coming. I promised Michael that if the same problems we fought hard to correct returned, I would seek a divorce.

Amid these problems, Nana died on Thanksgiving Day of 2001. She was 103 years old. Although my grandmother had an insurance policy, there was a clause at the bottom that I had never read. According to the clause, if you lived to be greater than 100 years old, the policy was void. She had outlived her policy, and the company would not honor it.

To make matters worse, a relative called me and shared the gossip that was rumbling amongst the family. There were comments like, "Auntie Odell did so much for her. Let's see how she takes care of her grandmother now." I interpreted that to mean that I should not ask anyone for money. This news was hurtful. Nana helped so many people in her lifetime. The gossip must have been true because no one asked if I needed assistance or offered to provide any. Fortunately, I received a donation from a friend who would eventually become my business partner. In addition, the owner and management staff of the computer company where I worked paid the expense for the repast at the church. I dropped two classes at the seminary to afford the remaining homegoing expenses. Because my grandmother was in a nursing home, she was not an active member of the church. However, Rev. Johnson, our pastor, agreed to officiate the homegoing service. Rev. Johnson preached her eulogy entitled "The Holiday Inn." The Holiday Inn represented my mother, father, and grandmother's days of transition. My mother's service was the day before Mother's Day; my father passed on St. Patrick's Day and my grandmother on Thanksgiving Day. Nana was cremated, and I kept her ashes in the house for three years before I honored her wish to have her ashes sprinkled in the same location as my mother's—Boston Harbor. The last person who loved me unconditionally, made provision for me, and believed in my aspirations was gone from my life. She often expressed her high hopes and expectations for my life. I am because of her.

WHO MOVED THE FINISH LINE?

After Nana's death, I immersed myself in my studies and church life. I was glad to have Rev. Johnson as a pastor. He infused a new passion for ministry, Black Liberation Theology, and Jesus into my life.

Hartford Seminary offered a two-week-long summer program titled "Congregational Studies" under the leadership of the Rev. Dr. Carl Dudley. Carl was my adviser in seminary school, and we developed a great friendship. I reveled at the chance to take another class with him. However, another student and I who were taking the course for credit overlooked a major requirement. Any student wishing to receive a letter grade and three academic credits had to write a 25-page paper and make a presentation. The paper was due in two weeks, and the assigned book was, Upon This Rock: The Miracles of a Black Church. This book was following me! We divided the chapters of the book. I remember having lunch with one of the other students, and he shared his reflections on the book. I took mental notes for my paper. I could not believe that this was recommended reading years ago. I submitted the paper on time and received a passing grade. In the fall, I would complete all my requirements; one more year left.

Upon completing the summer program, I was looking forward to wrapping up my last year at the Hartford Seminary. Rev. Lammie had transferred to Yale Divinity School two years earlier, and we were both scheduled to graduate the same year. I petitioned Hartford Seminary to include a class in Black Liberation Theology in its curriculum. The dean agreed. There were six of us gathered in a classroom for the course when in walked a man bigger than life wearing cowboy boots. He didn't smile. He just sat down in front of the class and introduced himself as Rev. Benjamin Watts, pastor of Shiloh Baptist Church in New London, Connecticut.

Rev. Watts lectured from the books of James Cone, Howard Thurman, and Cain Hope Felder. One night during the class break, the students discussed asking him to alter his teaching style. His lectures were not engaging, and we wanted him to share his personal reflections and stories of these theologians and struggles with the formation of Black Liberation Theology. I was nominated to speak to him since it was my idea to have the class. I convinced another classmate, Garland Higgins, to accompany me. We walked shoulder to shoulder for strength and located him in the coffee room. My knees were shaking. I looked up and started stuttering. Rev. Watts seemed to stand 8-feet tall when we approached him.

"Reverend Watts, the entire class has nominated me to ask you to change your teaching style," I said.

I could hear the floor shake and rumble. Rev. Watts turned around and stared at us but didn't utter a word. I continued, telling him that his perspective would be invaluable because he knew these theologians we were studying and had first-hand knowledge of their thoughts, struggles and triumphs that were not in the book.

Rev. Watts continued to stare at us, and I took it as our cue to leave. Garland and I backed out of the kitchen and bolted back to the classroom.

"What did he say?" our classmates asked.

"Nothing," Garland and I replied in unison.

Moments later, Rev. Watts returned to the room. He slowly sat down and looked at each person in the class. He closed his lecture notes and began teaching and engaging us in dialogue. My class members and I exhaled.

I learned more about these theologians than most students. Rev. Watts had a plethora of insight and personal knowledge. Nonetheless, my senior year in seminary was stressful trying to meet the demands to graduate at the same time that my crumbling marriage was coming to an end.

One morning, as I was preparing for work, Michael called me downstairs. When I walked into the living room, two police officers were standing there with note pads. The front door was wide open. I noticed my nosy neighbors standing on the curb, looking into our doorway with puzzled expressions. One of the police officers said my husband called them and stated that I hit him. The officer looked down at me and raised his head to stare at my husband. For a moment, I had flashbacks to the last two years. I took a deep breath.

"No, I didn't hit my husband. I finally hit him back," I said.

Both officers looked surprised, and my husband had a smirk on his face. Two months later, in October 2003, on the day I graduated from seminary school, Michael moved out. Neither he nor any of my family in Connecticut attended my graduation ceremony. Thankfully, my brother Ben drove up from Virginia to support me on this special day. Once Michael left the house, Ben gave me a comforting hug and smile. Again, I had conflicted feelings, but I was not going to let anything, or anyone, ruin my day. I remained quiet about my pain and dissolving marriage and graduated with a false smile, scared about my future.

My son Jonathan and adviser, the Rev. Dr. Carl Dudley, placed the graduation stole over my head. After walking off the stage, there stood Rev. Watts waiting for me and smiling. I thought he didn't like me for challenging his teaching style. I started to keep walking, but I knew better. I shook his hand and thanked him. Before I could walk away, he told me that the seminary had appointed him as the new director of the Black Ministries Program. While holding my hand, he offered me the position of teacher's assistant for the BMP Program. I was shocked! Thinking this was a mistake, I reminded him who I was.

"I know," he replied, laughing. "Anyone brave enough to challenge me is someone who can work for me."

God had validated my ministry on this day, and I knew He would be present and care for me during this challenging and confusing time in my life. Although I was proud to be offered this opportunity, which I accepted, I returned to an empty house with two children and life as a single mother. Sitting alone in my room, I wondered aloud whether this was really God's plan for my life. Had I exhausted all possibilities to save my marriage? The following morning, I called Michael, intending to ask him to turn around and come home. But before I could speak the words, I felt the ground beneath me rumble, the room sway like turbulent waters. The moment I hung up the phone, the trembling stopped. When I attempted to make the call later that day, the same thing happened. It was as if the house was turned upside down while every bone in my body shook. It was then I realized, yes, this is God's plan. God is present and wants me to have faith. A year later, Michael and I were divorced. The marriage chapter ended, and God's plan was about to begin.

CHAPTER 6

INTERRUPTION: SINGLE PARENTING

I WOKE UP TO THE BRIGHT sun shining on my face through the skylight in my bedroom. It had been a month since my divorce was final, and I still found myself lying flat on my side of this queen-size bed. It seemed like there was an invisible electronic shield in the middle of the bed that was preventing me from rolling over. Tonight, I promised myself I would adjust the pillows and sleep in the middle of the bed.

Resisting the will to move, I could smell breakfast coming from downstairs. Thankful to have a daughter who can make coffee and cook pancakes, I remained frozen on my side of the bed. I did not realize that God had answered my prayers. I was free to reclaim a healthy and safe lifestyle for myself and my children. Unfortunately, being divorced was not the plan. I knew there would be financial struggles, but I had ignored looking at the bills, creating a budget, and adopting a new attitude for the past week.

Dreading another Saturday, I struggled to wear the mask that said, "We will be OK." Instead, I laid there feeling sorry for myself, and the tears began to fall. I turned my head to find a dry spot on my pillow, and it seemed like a bolt of lightning jolted me. I could hear my voice of reason saying, "Wake up! Get up and stop feeling sorry for yourself! I promised you that I would be with you and will never forsake you." Then I remembered God blessed me with a rather unique upbringing by three strong Black women with opposite beliefs and backgrounds. Nana worked as a live-in domestic caretaker. Her personal belongings were reduced to a small bedroom with a full-size bed, a small closet, a white wooden five-drawer dresser, and costume jewelry. She owned five red dresses, one dress coat, two red pocketbooks, and three pairs of shoes. Nana was always happy, possessing a joyful, contagious laugh. She owned only the essentials and made sure her family was financially secure. On Sundays, she made quality time for us and introduced me to church and God. Momma Doe provided family cultural traditions. Growing up with all my cousins and the matriarchs and patriarchs of the Thompson family taught me to be Black and proud, which is likely why I am passionate about Black Liberation Theology and did not hesitate to introduce Cornell Dining to Momma Doe's cooking during the Black History Dinner. My mother could not cook soul food but was an excellent culinary chef who gave me culture: exposure to museums, Broadway shows, books, education, international travel, and life outside the Dorchester neighborhood called "Four Corners," where I grew up. Reflecting on these three women, I realized that it was now my responsibility to harness all their teachings, love and insight, and raise my children, trusting that God has a plan.

ENTREPRENEURSHIP

Our church wanted to develop a computer lab, and I was interested in helping but lacked the necessary technical expertise. Then Tony introduced me to James. James and I set out to work on the church computer lab. When that effort stalled, I learned of another opportunity to operate an established computer lab in Springfield, Massachusetts. James and I became business partners to move forward with that opportunity, which provided a supplemental income that was extremely helpful. I maintained my employment in Windsor, and we continued worshipping at Bethel AME in Bloomfield. It seemed like I was always traveling on I-95 N for some reason or another.

On a return visit to a work assignment at a small bio-tech pharmaceutical company, while on lunch break, the IT director offered me a full-time position. My salary would double, the commute was closer, and the benefits were fabulous. I remember hesitating to consider the offer because science was my weakness. I barely understood some of the conversations during the IT training sessions. The IT director convinced me that although the staff knew the science, they needed assistance understanding the technology, which was my strength. In addition, the staff required immediate training on new Food and Drug Administration regulations regarding drug submissions, which I could provide. James gave me the courage to accept the position by reminding me of my prayers.

"I don't understand you people of faith who pray to God for a miracle, and when it shows up, you question it," he said. "If it's a gift from God, you'll be successful."

So, in June 2004, I began earning a great salary with benefits, and my financial struggles were over. What wasn't over were abdominal pains I had suffered off and on for a while. The night before I was scheduled to attend a weeklong conference in Washington, D.C., the pain in my abdomen returned. This time it was excruciating and would not subside. Ignoring that these were the same pains I previously experienced, I decided they were due to stress and made the trip. Alonzo flew into D.C. for the week; however, instead of having dinner with him, I was rushed to the emergency room. The doctor informed me that I had a cyst on my ovary, and they needed to operate immediately. I begged the D.C. doctor to let me return to Connecticut to follow up with my doctor there, but she denied the request, assuring me that I would be unable to walk two feet before I collapsed. After confirmation my health insurance would cover this "out-of-network" operation, I had surgery and stayed in the hospital for a week. However, even after being discharged from the hospital, I could not travel home for another month. My old college roommate Jodi, who lived in Washington, D.C., made room for me in her spare bedroom, and I stayed with her until I could safely travel back to Connecticut. When I returned home, I still had a job!

TIME FOR A MAKEOVER

During the next couple of months, I rearranged the house, purchased a red couch for the living room, a flat-screen TV that hung over the fireplace, and bought myself a new bed. I gave the old one to my daughter. The next morning, I woke up in the middle of my new queen-size pillow-top bed smiling. I was committed to reactivating my membership with Delta Sigma Theta Sorority, Inc., joining the New Haven Alumnae Chapter and becoming active again. At the same time, I enrolled Jackie in the Delta youth program. She was being mentored and remotivated. Jonathan enjoyed having all the older girls at the house.

That summer, I surprised the kids with a weeklong vacation to Ocho Rios, Jamaica, at the same resort Brenda and I visited months before. Brenda's daughter accompanied Jackie, Jonathan and me. I had saved my money and was committed to giving my children a wonderful week in Jamaica. The first thing I did was coordinate an excursion for every day of the week.

While sitting at the breakfast table with three teenagers one morning, I realized that the men at the resort did not approach me as they had the previous year when it was just Brenda and me. Nonetheless, I met a cool local who owned a shop on the island. I was going to find time to have Odell fun without the teens.

The week was great! I felt good that I was able to see the smiles return to my children's faces. We took plenty of pictures to remember this vacation.

Upon returning to the states, we prepared to attend family reunions in Washington, D.C. and San Francisco. Unfortunately, Jackie had been selected to participate in the advanced academic summer program at Choate Rosemary High School and could not leave for the summer. Again, I was feeling like my mother by traveling with the family. The Rogers-Thompson-Dabney Family Reunion was great, and it was refreshing to reconnect with family. While in San Francisco, I attended Glide Memorial Church and was captivated by the church's ministry and social justice life. I knew in my spirit that I needed to belong to a church not governed by 18th-century ministry guidelines. On the plane ride home, I began thinking about the various changes I needed to make in my church life.

SPEED DATING

My children often encouraged me to meet new people and convinced Brenda to take me out more. Brenda persuaded me to get dressed and meet her at the Elks Club in New Haven one night. She had secretly arranged to have me meet several guys at 20-minute speed dating intervals. When I arrived at the club, Brenda was already sitting at the table, surrounded by three chairs. Brenda introduced me to the first guy to arrive. This dude did not have any teeth and was wearing ugly shoes. That conversation did not last much longer than the greetings. Three minutes later, another man arrived. After the fourth introduction, I finally caught on to Brenda's plan. The seventh man in this speed dating soiree appeared, flashing a full set of teeth and wearing nice shoes. He sat down, and the conversation went well until it seemed like the needle on the album screeched.

"You don't ever have to worry about calling my house and having a woman answer. I live with my momma," he said.

He invited me to the Apollo Theater in Harlem for a concert, complete with backstage VIP passes. However, he wanted to know if I had a problem riding in the front seat of his limo while he drove his clients. The final clincher was when he looked over at my drink and said, "How many of these do you need to make you feel special?" When he went to the bar to buy us another drink, I walked away.

Was this my dating life? As I was standing near the pool table at the Elks shaking my head at the disappointing night, from the corner of my eye, I caught a glimpse of a fine Black man walking my way. He had a beautiful smile, wore a black leather coat and shiny black leather boots. He walked with a sexy swag. I thought, "Finally!" I had never seen this man before, but he was gorgeous. He stood in front of me! I could smell his sexy cologne, and I melted. I smiled and inhaled his essence.

"What's your name?" he asked.

I opened my mouth and began to stutter. I made the sound, O, and got stuck. It took what seemed like two minutes to say, "OOOOOOO . . . Odell." He stepped back and smiled.

"Damn, that looked like it hurt," he said.

I put down my drink, found Brenda, and told her I was leaving the Elks.

Driving home, I was mortified. But then the Holy Spirit spoke to me.

"I hold your tongue. You will use it for me or not at all," I heard.

The next day, I thanked Brenda for helping me to recapture my sense of style and belief in myself. But I vowed never to return to the Elks Club. Sunday morning, I was back in church wearing my new confident and colorful, coordinated outfit. This time, I was following the will of God for my life, knowing God has a way of getting my attention.

TWIN SISTERS

I was fortunate to reconnect with my ex-husband's twin daughters, Margarette and Arynce, who lived in New York. I met the twins eight years earlier when they came to Connecticut for a day visit. Jackie and Jonathan were toddlers. I was excited to meet them finally. Both girls had their father's strong facial features. I told them that their father and I divorced, and I was raising their siblings. I asked permission to be included in their life and wanted us to have a relationship. They agreed, and for the next six years, it was my mission to ensure Jackie and Jonathan had a relationship with their sisters. Their family was wonderful, open, and receptive to all of us. We drove to New York and joined their families for Thanksgiving dinners, birthday celebrations, graduations, and Margarette's wedding. My daughter was excited to have big sisters. Jonathan just felt surrounded by women.

HIGH SCHOOL WAS NOT THIS HARD

After Jonathan's 8th grade graduation, Alonzo called and offered Jonathan a chance to leave the state for three weeks. He was coaching a basketball camp in northern Virginia and gave Jonathan a scholarship to attend. Jackie and I packed his bags and we drove him to camp. At the same time, Jackie and I were looking forward to a quieter time before school started.

In the fall, Jackie and Jonathan enrolled in the same high school, Metropolitan Business Academy. Jonathan reconnected with Marcel and formed new friendships with other classmates, Damar and Kenny. These were the guys he called his brothers. They were always together, either at our house or theirs. If he was not with them, he was with his cousins Skeeter and Zeke or Howie T. They were all the same age. Jonathan was more social than Jackie, and the house seemed to have more energy and life with his friends coming and going. I was committed to allowing my house to be the home their friends would feel comfortable visiting, enjoying the pool, deck and the basketball hoop in the front yard. It worked. There was always music playing, dancing, and joyful noise.

Every summer while they were in high school, I arranged to have both my kids enrolled in a summer program. One summer, Jonathan grudgingly attended a program at Yale University that Jackie had participated in the previous summer. It was a six-week program, but he never asked for money. Being the concerned mother, I needed to know why.

"I am using my skills by playing poker with the international students," he explained. He learned to use a family tradition taught by his great-grandmother as a hustle.

Starting in the fall of that year, I regularly heard irritating, loud rap music vibrating from the family room. The boys called themselves Da-Law, and Da-Law was always dancing, rapping, and making noise.

My mother hid her health problems from me growing up and I wanted to break that cycle. I made my children promise we would never lie about our health, and they would ask me any questions about life in case I forgot to educate them during their teenage years. Then one day during dinner Jackie asked if they were test-tube babies or the product of in vitro fertilization. Confused by the question, I confirmed they were both born out of love and natural conception. I explained Jackie was a needy child and somewhat annoying. She often wedged herself between her father and me and woke us early every Sunday morning by crawling in bed with us. It was then I decided she needed a sibling, and that's why Jonathan was born. They laughed at the story.

"I was planned," Jackie said.

Then Jonathan responded, "Yeah, but I was more planned."

Despite their arguing, Jonathan was the bridge for Jackie and me. Whenever she and I had arguments or disagreements, Jonathan helped resolve our differences. Jackie was a true big sister to her brother. Growing up, she would tell the babysitters to feed her first, and she would care for her brother.

Jackie rarely got into trouble in school or had disciplinary issues. I let them convince me to organize and have a leadership role in their school's Parent Teacher Association (PTA). Having two teenagers in high school was challenging, especially when my job demanded that I travel. While I was away, to ensure they were safe and behaving, I relied on my neighbor who worked in criminal justice and my sorority sister to make occasional unannounced walk-throughs at my house. It worked!

In Jackie's senior year, she decided to skip school while driving my car. Her teacher, Mr. Raynor, called and told me she had come to school, signed in, and left. He asked Jonathan to call his sister, but Jackie did not answer the phone. After trying to reach Jackie several times on her cellphone and leaving threatening voice messages, I gave up. I remember calling Angel from work, and we laughed that her godchild did not know how to cut school without getting busted. I did not want to cut off her phone because I wanted Jackie to call if she needed help. Therefore, I reported my car stolen, and I told Jonathan to call her and leave that message on her phone. Thirty minutes later, Jackie pulled up in the driveway as if she had attended school.

"I have been good in school all these years. I should be entitled to participate in senior skip day," she argued.

I recalled feeling the same restrictions growing up but still took the keys to the car for a week.

That same year, Metropolitan Business Academy received a new assistant principal who seemed adamant about expelling Black boys from school. On the last day of school before spring break, Jonathan, Marcel, and Damar were standing on school property after dismissal when Jonathan got into his first fight. Since the fight happened on school property, the assistant principal called Jonathan into the office and was attempting to expel him. Mr. Raynor texted me and coached me on how to respond to this upcoming phone call. If expelled, Jonathan could no longer attend this magnet school. Mr. Raynor told me to ask for a nine-day, out-of-school suspension instead of the proposed ten days, which allowed him to return to school. When the assistant principal phoned, I knew what to say to save my son from being expelled, and he was suspended for nine days.

While Jonathan was home, he had to clean the entire house from top to bottom. During this time, Mr. Raynor called to inform me that all high school juniors needed to complete and pass their exams before entering their senior year. If Jonathan was not present, he would not be eligible to advance to the 12th grade. I arranged for him to attend school solely to take his exams and then return home. On the last day of exams, the assistant principal once again called. I quickly checked my phone for a heads-up from Mr. Raynor, but nothing was there. As the assistant principal informed me about Jonathan, I could hear teachers in the background laughing and debating who would share the news about my son.

This time, Jonathan's girlfriend broke up with him. In retaliation, his posse, the Da-Law, recorded a YouTube video showing the destruction of the stuffed dog she had gifted him for Valentine's Day. Da-Law were wearing red bandanas on their faces and videoed the mutilation of this poor stuffed dog in our family room. The entire school was disturbed upon viewing this video, which also caused his ex-girlfriend the utmost embarrassment.

The teachers asked Jackie to make her brother take the video off YouTube. However, Jackie was still holding a grudge about her brother ratting her out for Senior Skip Day. She insisted the school call me instead. Jonathan knew I would always defend him, and he encouraged them to make the call. I could hear the teachers laughing in the background. When they told me that Jonathan and his friends were wearing red bandanas and filmed the video in my house, a question came to mind.

"If the boys were wearing red bandanas on their faces, how could they prove it was my son?" I asked.

"Well, Odell, we know it was videotaped in your house because of the family pictures of Jackie and Jonathan hanging on the back wall and of you with your sorority sisters. Your sorority is the only one we allow to come to the school for voter registration," the teacher responded.

I could overhear one of the teachers saying that because Jonathan posted the video at home and was already suspended, the school could only inform me about the incident. It could not administer any disciplinary action. I made Jackie take her brother to his ex-girlfriend's classroom and apologize to her.

Jonathan and Da-Law made me step up my parenting game. I came home one Saturday afternoon to find Da-Law sitting on the couch holding red bandanas. When I inquired why they were all sitting on my couch, they replied, "no reason." I knew something was going on, and I promised them that if I ever found out something different, they were going to regret it. When Da-Law showed up at the house again, I waited until they all had on their new Jordan sneakers and were playing basketball in the driveway. I pulled out the water hose and drenched them all. I went in the house, turned up the speakers, and blasted James Brown's song, "Payback." I knew they were angry with me, but there was nothing they could do. Now I understood motherhood. Kids cannot win or ever embarrass the parent. There will be consequences. I could hear Jackie laughing from her bedroom for hours. It wasn't over yet.

Later that night, Jackie sat on the couch in the living room for two hours, eating popcorn as if she had a front-row seat in a suspense and drama movie. As a single parent who was shorter than everyone in the house, I had to find creative ways to correct inappropriate behavior. Growing up, Jonathan was the runner; he would run and hide the moment he saw a belt. He sometimes hid on the side of the refrigerator or under the bed, making it difficult to find him. He was now too big to hide but still a runner. It must have been a good performance because Jackie laughed for the entire two hours. All she could say was, "Glad it's not me."

Whenever I needed to reinforce punishments, I would solicit the assistance of godfather Tony and business partner James. They came to the house and took Jonathan out for four hours. Later, he complained that the lectures from Uncle Tony and Mr. James were excruciating. That summer, James and Tony recommended I enroll Jonathan into a video program at Fairfield University because he enjoyed making videos.

Following their advice, Marcel rode with me to drop Jonathan off at Fairfield. During our drive, I pleaded with my son to behave. As we waited for the elevator in the lobby of his dormitory, we noticed some students staring at us and quietly whispering to one another. I did not see any other Black boys in the program and began getting nervous. Marcel asked me to wait in the car. My heart began to beat even faster. I was thinking that Jonathan was going to be kicked out of the program before it began. Marcel returned to the car and confirmed everything was safe. I texted Jonathan to call me once he unpacked. Before we reached the highway, I received a call saying, "Ma, I didn't do anything." The boys in the hallway had seen the posted video he made with Da-Law wearing the red bandanas and complimented him on his editing skills. During part of the video, Jonathan says, "God makes it rain, and I can make snow," as he and his friends threw the white stuffing in the air and watched it slowly tumble to the floor. So, Jonathan called to assure me that I need not worry as he would be fine. It seems he was right because the next day, upperclassmen invited him to join their video competition team, which cost him $50 to join. His team won the competition, and I did not need to provide him with any money for the entire six-week program. When I picked him up, he was wearing new jeans, a pair of Jordan's and a small 14K gold earring in his ear.

CHAPTER 7
INTERRUPTION: I TURNED INTO MY MOTHER

IN 2008, JACKIE GRADUATED HIGH SCHOOL and insisted on attending college out of state. She enrolled at Florida A&M University (FAMU) in Tallahassee, Florida, to major in civil engineering. As a mother, it was my responsibility to help my children explore their dreams. But instead, I pushed an HBCU on Jackie. I wanted her to have the same experience as I did at Howard University. In hindsight, I had become my mother, pushing my experience and thoughts about college instead of letting it be her choice.

IN AND OUT
In Jackie's first year of college, she asked for a tattoo. I firmly said "no" to her request because of my feelings that it would jeopardize her employment opportunities. Weeks later, the bank statement came to the house. I read the statement but overlooked the charge that read "Tallahassee Tattoo Parlor." Jonathan already knew she had a tattoo and asked, "Mom, did you really read the bank statement?" Since he was not detail-oriented, I knew he was trying to subtly tell me something. I looked at the statement again, and there it was in big print—a $50 charge at Tallahassee Tattoo Parlor. Jonathan then convinced me to look at Jackie's Facebook page on his computer. There it was. Jackie had my nickname for her, "Princess," tattooed on her shoulder; she decided not to be called "Pumpkin," and we settled on "Princess." I threatened Jonathan not to tell his sister that I knew about the tattoo until she returned home. When she returned for the summer, I

waited until it was 90 degrees outside to convince Jackie to help me clean up the yard. She wore long sleeves, and I suggested she wear a different shirt, but Jackie insisted she was fine. Twenty minutes later, sweat was pouring down her face, and her shirt was soaked. Jonathan stood in the window laughing, finally having his chance at sibling revenge. Jackie eventually ran into the house and pulled off her shirt. I followed her and looked shocked when I saw her tattoo. Jonathan cracked up laughing on the floor and enjoyed watching me torture his sister. Jackie finally confessed.

"I know you didn't want me to have a tattoo, but I got your favorite name for me, so I thought you would like it. Surprise!" she said.

Unfortunately, Jackie did not enjoy the HBCU. Against my advice, she did not return to FAMU and wanted to change her major. She asked for the opportunity to make her own career choice and school selection.

In 2010, Jonathan graduated from high school and decided to attend Eastern Connecticut State University. It took months before he finally realized that basketball was not a major but a sport you played in college. He enrolled in the school of liberal arts and had one year to declare a major. I was looking forward to living alone. However, as I moved one child onto campus, the oldest returned and was back in the house.

Every morning when I left the house for work, Jackie was lying in bed watching television and eating my food. The first month, I was sympathetic, and in the second month, nothing changed. I noticed my attitude toward her was short, and our conversations seemed like sermons. Me telling her to make a decision, either school or work, but she was not going to lay up in my house using my electricity, hot water, and watching cable every day. As the holiday was approaching, Jonathan was home from school for a month, and now there were two young adults in the house. I gave Jonathan a pass, but Jackie's time was up.

During my shopping in Home Depot for extra Christmas lights, I noticed a Digital Indoor Timer device designed to turn lights on and off at a particular time. I sent Jackie to the store for groceries, and I connected the timer to her TV and light switch in her bedroom. After a specific time, both would turn off. When Jackie returned to her room after dinner and used the remote to turn on the TV, John and I were in the living room watching a movie, and we heard, "Hey, what happened to my lights?" She walked into the living room and noticed the electricity was working, and then it hit her.

"Get a job or go to school," I looked up and reiterated. "I am not going to allow you these liberties for free."

Jackie began coming out of her room and spending more time with us. Two weeks later, she had a job working in a local grocery store and could catch the bus to and from work. Although she was working, it didn't stop me from convincing her to return to college before she ended up too comfortable.

Before Jonathan returned to school, Momma Doe passed. It was an emotional and sad homegoing. Both my parents and Nana had passed, and now Momma Doe. Over her lifetime, she had opened her home and heart to raise other people's children. We all returned to say, I love you and thank you. I was fortunate to have Jackie and Jonathan around so they could continue to hear all the childhood stories about growing up with Momma Doe. Secretly, we called her Clint Eastwood because she never missed her target.

Weeks later, Jonathan returned to school for the fall semester and was passing, but I felt he was partying too much on campus. It was now Jackie's turn to share his activities on Facebook. A few months later they both approached me about joining the military. Jonathan's friend Damar had joined the National Guard after high school instead of attending college and was trying to convince Jonathan to join him. While Damar often said it was hard work, he also said he knew he made the right decision as the army provided stability and a chance to travel and do extraordinary things. He shared his experiences with Jonathan, prompting Jonathan to join. Damar was both excited and nervous about Jonathan joining the Guard. Every mother knows her child, and Jonathan did not like to listen. He tended to be in the wrong place at the wrong time. In the service, that could get you killed or dismissed. Nonetheless, it was apparent that Damar had made a positive impression because Jonathan was excited about joining the service.

Jackie, on the other hand, wanted to pursue the Air Force. One of my sorority sisters tutored Jackie to help her pass the exam, and she did. However, because of her asthma, she did not pass the physical and her application to join the Air Force was denied. Meanwhile, Jonathan passed the exam and the physical. However, when asked whether he had ever smoked marijuana, he decided not to lie about his health and said "yes." When I asked what happened, he said he had raised his right hand and promised to tell the truth. His "yes" response was the wrong answer, and Jonathan's application to join the service was denied. I called his recruiter for advice, but our options were limited. I also phoned a cousin who was a retired lieutenant colonel. He graciously agreed to submit a letter to the review board. However, the letter was unsuccessful in overturning the decision.

The disappointing news for both my children was heartbreaking. Both of their dreams were shattered, and we cried. It was a difficult time. I felt helpless watching my children's options dwindle.

Jonathan had a great recruiter who helped him to stop smoking weed and decrease his drinking. Jonathan also met the other students enrolled in the National Guard on campus, who helped him become more focused in life. He eventually called Damar and shared the bad news but vowed to find something else to do, a classic Jonathan response. He was not going to let that denial be his legacy. This experience changed them both. Jackie started spending more time with her boyfriend, and Jonathan began exploring music. His friends began calling him Coop.

In the fall of 2012, I noticed Jonathan's grades slipping as he showed more interest in music than studying. At the same time, I was working in my career, making good money and teaching as an adjunct at three local colleges. When Coop came home for a break, I informed him of my decision to stop taking out loans for mediocre grades. We discussed options—coming back to New Haven and living in the house was not one of them. Too many young Black teenagers were being shot, and the city didn't feel safe. Every long weekend or break, someone new showed up to the house looking for "Coop" to rap or mix beats in the family room. Unlike my early childhood experience, Coop was not sitting on the bed asking to join the group; he was the group. I admit I did not like the sound or lyrics that Coop was making. In one song, entitled "Area Code," I heard, "I'm from the 2-0, the 2-0." I yelled out, "Where's the 3?"

Our area code is 203. That's why I hate that song; it was incomplete.

Jackie convinced me to buy Jonathan a video camera for Christmas. As with most things my children asked me to buy, I blindly agreed. What a year! Coop posted everything on Facebook, and Jackie made sure I saw every video of him and his new friends, who had named their rap group the Wavy Gang, dancing and rapping. I sent a comment telling him to remove the videos. Jonathan responded, "Mom, it's my page, and if you continue to make comments, I will unfriend you." So, I started calling him to complain. He eventually refused to answer my calls. As a single mother, I learned to be highly creative. I called the phone company and reported the phone was lost again and asked them to cut off the phone until I located it. Within the next five minutes, I received a call from an unknown number. Coop was calling.

"OK, mom, you win," he said.

He completed his second year of college and came home. Remembering what I did with Jackie and the lights, he took a different approach.

Now both children were back in the house working hourly jobs. This time was the moment of truth for me. I had different dreams for all of us, and I was beginning to wonder how I failed my children.

Coop was working two jobs, UPS at night and casual status Yale Dining, and enrolled in Gateway Community College in New Haven. He was transitioning into music/video production, which was his true calling. I offered to send Jackie to live with her godmother Tanya in Maryland, so she would not feel stuck and unable to pursue a dream. She declined the offer and began working part time culinary positions. After four part-time jobs in the culinary world, Jackie discovered she had a passion for working behind the house—in the kitchen. Two years after returning from college and searching for her identity, Jackie became pregnant.

Honestly, I was not happy about her decision to become a single parent. I knew that her life would be difficult and challenging, but she would not listen. During her first four months of pregnancy, I did not tell anyone Jackie was pregnant. I was angry and disgusted with Jackie and often voiced how her pregnancy would affect her future. But the Holy Spirit quickly reminded me that my parents had not been married and look at my life.

I stopped being disappointed with my daughter and accepted the future. I was going to be a grandmother.

My son moved out of his room and converted the family room into his own personal suite. He repainted his room for his niece and looked forward to becoming Uncle Coop.

Coop asked if his friend Coqui could stay with us for the summer. I remember Coqui telling me he never ate dinner with his family or felt as safe and loved as he did that summer. Coqui and Coop tried painting houses around town. They were both horrible at the job and needed transportation. Of course, I made sure they arrived at the location on time and picked them up after work. Looking back, I should have kicked myself for being so gullible. Coop asked if he could use my car because they had to paint a house at 6 a.m., and the drive was an hour long. He told me I would need to catch the train home from my job because he and Coqui would still be working. After a few choice words in different octaves of my voice, they never worked another paint job again.

MY TURN TO DREAM

While working as the teacher's assistant at Hartford Seminary on Saturdays, I noticed a job posting on the board for a director of ministry position at Mount Aery Baptist Church in Bridgeport. I was intrigued by the position. I realized my children were going to live their lives and make their own decisions. Therefore, it was my turn to live my dreams. I phoned my mentor Rev. McCorn and asked him if he knew of Pastor Anthony Bennett and the Mount Aery Baptist Church. He highly recommended the position and Bennett.

"You remember the book I gave you years ago, Upon This Rock?" Pastor McCorn said. "My fraternity brother Anthony Bennett is in the book."

I began to feel that this book was haunting me, and I should read it, but I still did not. Pastor McCorn cautioned me that although working in ministry was rewarding, the salary would not be close to what I was earning working in the secular world.

During my first interview with Pastor Bennett, he asked me if I'd read Upon This Rock. I laughed and said yes, but conveniently omitted the details. Pastor Bennett hired me for what was my first professional position in full-time ministry. On my second day on the job, he asked if I could attend a round table discussion with a few lay church members interested in understanding the benefits of attending seminary school. Pastor Bennett had a conflict in his schedule and felt I could handle the panel discussion since I worked at the seminary. There were members of his previous church in Brooklyn, New York, St. Paul Community Baptist Church, who were attending the roundtable. He assured me that the renowned liberation theologist Rev. Dr. Johnny Ray Youngblood, was unable to attend. I knew that Dr. Youngblood was one of the people in Upon This Rock. I was nervous and cracking up on the inside. As I was driving up to Hartford Seminary, Pastor Bennett phoned and told me that his meeting had been canceled and he was en route but wanted me to lead the discussion with the six church members. I called Angel and expressed both anxiety and humor about God having jokes at my expense. While standing in the seminary lobby waiting for the six church members to arrive, a 48-passenger coach bus pulled up, and Black folks started piling out. I counted at least 35 people before they reached the front door. Then I locked eyes on the pastor who was not supposed to be present, the Rev. Dr. Youngblood, who had written Upon This Rock. My heart began to beat faster and sweat was pouring from my face. In addition to being a published author, Dr. Youngblood was an outstanding pastor in an 8,000-member urban church, a powerful preacher, and a recognized faith-based community organizer. He had been studied and discussed in seminary and divinity schools around the globe. When I locked eyes on him, I thought my fake eyelashes were on my cheekbone. I phoned Pastor Bennett and informed him that Rev. Dr. Youngblood was present. He replied, "I'm on my way, don't worry."

I quickly rearranged the tables from a round table setup to one resembling the classroom setting in which I felt comfortable teaching. When the church folks arrived, I mentally thought of them as students sitting in a BMP class. Shortly after the introductions, Rev. Watts, Pastor Bennett, and the dean of Hartford Seminary filed into the room. They were present to pay respect to Rev. Youngblood.

I introduced myself and began sharing my background. One of the church members asked if I always knew I wanted to teach in seminary. I then began sharing the story of "Benny and the Jets," and laughter broke out everywhere. It was going well. Standing in the corner were both of my employers, Rev. Watts and Pastor Bennett. Talk about stress. Then Rev. Youngblood himself asked the dreaded question: "What section of the book inspired you the most?" I felt like I had stopped breathing. I knew better than to fudge a response. I glanced over at the wall where my employers and the dean were standing. The next words out of my mouth had to be the truth. Therefore, I admitted to only reading half of the book but shared the feedback from the other students taking the class that summer. Rev. Youngblood seemed to appreciate the truth, but I could not tell if Pastor Bennett would rescind the job offer or make my new career miserable because I omitted the truth about reading the book. After the session ended, both Pastor Bennett and Rev. Watts congratulated me on a job well done. I was feeling empowered and proud to be a part of this team. I went home that night and felt my contribution to the seminary and Mount Aery was deeply respected and appreciated.

I continued working in full-time ministry for five years before transitioning into other career opportunities. During those five years, I convinced a church deacon to come out of retirement to assist Mount Aery in becoming the first site in Connecticut to host the Children's Defense Fund Freedom School. It supported children and young adults in excelling and making significant contributions to improve their families and communities. We also partnered with the city of Bridgeport in a federal grant preparing residents for careers in green jobs and built a computer training lab, which Pastor Bennett called the "Liberation Lab." Working for Mount Aery was not always easy, but it was spiritually rewarding. My finances would last for three months, and I began interviewing with a goal to secure employment by July 2012. I learned that I had a strong passion for assisting adults in reinventing themselves for new viable career options that would lead to solid employment.

BACK TO WINCHESTER AVENUE

In June 2012, a new non-profit opened in New Haven in Science Park, a redeveloped area of New Haven. The non-profit, ConnCAT (Connecticut Center for Arts and Technology) was a job training center, which provided programs to give unemployed and under-employed adults the skills needed to secure meaningful employment. I interviewed for the position of manager of adult training. Although the interview seemed promising, and the company's mission would be rewarding, it would mean a reduction in income. The president said he would inform all candidates of his decision within a month. A month passed, and I had not heard from the school. I took a risk and sent an email asking if the position had been filled. The president responded with an apology for the delay and told me that after interviewing me he needed to restructure his staffing model and then take the new plan back to the board for approval. Instead of offering me the manager's position, he created a job based on my skillset for a career pathway manager. It was a position that would support the students and help them professionally prepare for employment as they worked through some personal challenges while enrolled in the program. Although ConnCAT was in Science Park, the street was Winchester Avenue. I was working walking distance from JoAnn and Roger's house. That was the job he offered me and the job I gratefully accepted. The following year, I was promoted.

In September 2013, Jackie gave birth to a baby girl. Everyone was enjoying their new roles of being Uncle Coop and I was now Nana.

The Rogers-Thompson-Dabney Family Reunion was held in June 2014 in Philadelphia, Pennsylvania. They asked me to preach during our Sunday service. I tried to convince them I was not a preacher but a lover of the Gospel. They would not accept no for an answer. That summer, while preparing my sermon, the Holy Spirit consumed my soul. I had never experienced such calmness and clarity during any preparation. It was true, the Holy Spirit really does inspire you with the scripture and message. The morning I preached for the family was the best experience of my life. When I returned home to Connecticut, I anxiously awaited my pastor's return from sabbatical to inform him that I was accepting the call to become a preacher. Pastor Bennett did not seem surprised but rather pleased about my decision. I believe he saw the gift while I had worked for him at the church as director of ministry development. On December 17, 2014, four other ministers and I were licensed to preach at Mount Aery Baptist Church in Bridgeport.

Occasionally, Jackie and Coop attended church with me. Coop began volunteering at the church in the audio ministry while working as a part-time security officer at ConnCAT and at UPS on weekends. One day he informed me that he had rented an apartment with some friends and was moving out. He moved 30 steps around the corner, but he was out of the house. I was never allowed to come by the house unless I phoned first. That situation lasted all of three months before he was again taking over the family room downstairs. All the traffic of friends and rap music returned. Coop and I discussed his moving out of the state. He dressed and looked like most of the young Black men in New Haven. I kept hearing the teacher's voice saying, "Jonathan didn't do anything wrong. He was just in the wrong place at the wrong time."

I arranged to have Coop enroll in a music school in Manhattan and live with my cousin Darsweil's son, Rande. However, in one year in New York, Coop had moved four times. I was unhappy with his constant moving and called his father for help. Michael's nephew Dwayne had an apartment in Harlem, a temporary solution but a lifesaver. Later, my sorority sister Donna arranged for him to get a permanent apartment in Brooklyn. Finally, the constant moving ended.

The family renting the room to Coop was great and watched over his well-being. If he neglected to come home, the mother would call Donna, and the chain of inquiry calls were made until he responded. Coop was spending additional time in the studio that summer. When school was not in session, he worked at FIKA coffee shop in Midtown Manhattan. He enjoyed living in Brooklyn and working in Manhattan. My visits to the city were déjà vu of my early years traveling from Pratt to Manhattan. One summer day, I visited him in New York at the coffee shop. He told me the story of a man who lived above the coffee shop and came into the shop every day. They enjoyed conversing with each other. My son told the man that he was also involved in music and attending school.

Coop told me about one of their more recent conversations. The man traveled to the West Coast on concert tours.

"Maybe you have heard of me," the man said to Coop. "My name is Tony Bennett."

"What's your stage name?" Coop replied.

"Tony Bennett, maybe you heard of my music and the last CD I made with Lady Gaga."

Coop told Tony Bennett to stay connected with Lady Gaga because she could make him famous.

Looking at me, Coop asked if I had ever heard of Tony Bennett. My mouth dropped in utter surprise, thinking how I had failed my child. I laughed at him for days.

"Really, Jonathan, Tony Bennett, the music legend," I replied. That was the year Tony Bennett and Lady Gaga hosted the Emmys and honored Stevie Wonder.

The following month, Coop got a job at a coffee shop in the Bryant Park area of Manhattan. He was subsequently promoted to a manager's position in the Financial District. School was now on hold. He began dating a Swedish chef who was in the United States on a work visa. She was tall and beautiful, with strong Swedish features. I was shocked, wondering how my son pulled her. She cooked for us in the morning and cleaned the kitchen. After their third trip home for Thanksgiving dinner, I knew school was off the table and began to understand why he was pursuing a full-time job with benefits. He was getting serious about dating, and his focus had shifted again. It was again time for me to focus on my life. I learned my children would make their own decisions in life, and I had to pursue my passion.

CHAPTER 8
INTERRUPTION: FAMILY IN CULINARY ARTS

IN JANUARY 2016, CONNCAT DESIGNED AND opened a culinary school. I was promoted to director of the culinary school. Deciding to pursue a culinary career, Jackie enrolled in culinary school. She was balancing her life as a single mother, full-time student and working part-time.

Four months into the culinary program, we hosted Friends and Family Day on Friday, April 13, 2016. Jackie insisted on having her brother present. Jonathan was still living and working in New York, and when I spoke to him on the phone, he told me he could not attend that Friday. I asked him if I changed the date to the 23rd could he attend. He replied, "Yes." I announced the date change to the class, and everyone responded favorably.

While he was home, Jonathan wanted to see his friend Damar, who was now months away from becoming a father. Jonathan and their friend Marcel were planning to buy the crib and become godparents. Marcel had started dating a new girl whose name he began mentioning at the house. My children were growing up, and life was looking good. Jackie, her daughter, and I picked Jonathan up from the train station, and we all had dinner together. My granddaughter was so happy to see her Uncle Coop. The following morning, the entire family was in the car. I took a selfie of all the smiles. I was proud of my family and looked forward to spending the day with them in the culinary school. We had a great day, and before class ended at 1:30 p.m., my coworker snapped a family picture of the three of us wearing our culinary whites. Jonathan had spent time connecting with the ConnCAT staff and sharing his new life successes in New York.

Coop always enjoyed placing his elbow on my head to remind me how short I was or how he was taller than the women in the house. The day ended, and Jackie and Coop took my car, and he drove her to work. He returned to pick me up from work, and we had dinner. Jonathan always wanted a good burger and beer. During dinner, we talked about his relationship with his girlfriend. She was returning to Sweden at the end of the month. I sensed he was heartbroken and not handling her departure well. I wanted to tell him to pack his bags and return to New York tonight. I wanted to say, "Go find her and figure out how you can secure a work visa and travel overseas with her." The words never came out of my mouth. Instead, I listened to him vent about love. He then asked me if he could return home and enroll in ConnCAT. My gut was saying no. I asked him to think about it and suggested that we just enjoy the night. The last place I wanted him was back in New Haven, where too many young Black men were being shot. Plus, he had finally found his groove in New York. For some reason, I never worried about him traveling between Brooklyn and Manhattan, only in New Haven.

Coop asked me if he could use the car because he wanted to see his cousin Zeke for his birthday and hang out with his cousin Skeeter, my sister Charlene's son. At first, I said no and suggested he make other plans. I reminded him of the last time I let him take my car with Skeeter, and they had hit a fire hydrant and lied about what happened. I could not afford another insurance claim and the accompanying deductible cost. I finally agreed to let Coop take the car. I could track my car via the app and texted him around midnight about his ETA. He responded shortly telling me not to worry. I finally fell asleep with the cellphone in my hand.

CHAPTER 9
INTERRUPTION: NOT MY SON

I FELT A VIBRATION ON THE bed and realized I had a call. Barely awake, glancing at the phone, the caller ID read Sarah. Immediately wondering if my son was home, I ignored the call, rolled out of bed, and staggered to my bathroom window. Peeping through the blinds, I noticed my car was not in the driveway. My anxiety level was rising. My son should be home by now. Before I could reach my bed to call him, the phone rang again. This time, the caller ID read Angel. Why were they calling me from Boston this time in the morning?

I shifted my concern to Sarah. Was she sick and in the hospital? "Oh no," I thought, "I should have answered the call." I answered Angel's call, anxious and worried.

"What's wrong?" I shouted into the receiver. "First Sarah, and now you at 1:30 in the morning. What is wrong?"

Before Angel could respond, Sarah was calling again. I asked Angel to hold and clicked over to the incoming call.

"What is going on?" I asked Sarah, realizing I sounded sharper than I intended. "You and Angel are both calling me at 1:30 in the morning!"

Sarah told me to hang up with Angel and asked whether Jackie was home. I said she was.

My concern was escalating.

Sarah said, "Sis, your son has been shot."

Sarah's call didn't make any sense. She lived in Boston. How would she know this information?

"Charlene called and told me to call you," Sarah continued.

My heart was beating a mile a minute and I was annoyed by her response. Why was I receiving calls from Boston about my son instead of Charlene being at my door?

"Sarah, I will call you later. I have to go."

I clicked over to Angel, repeating the news that Jonathan had been shot and I needed to hang up.

There was an eerie moment of silence. Angel and I had been friends for over 38 years, and I could sense there was more to her silence.

"Is that what she told you?" Angel asked.

I answered, yes. By this time, I was too upset to inquire about what sounded like skepticism in Angel's voice. I dismissed it but felt uncomfortable. I promised to call her back with an update.

"Jackie, Jackie, wake up!" I called out.

Were the screams coming from my bedroom?

Putting on clothes, I found a hoodie and kept yelling Jackie's name until she responded. My half-asleep daughter appeared in my bedroom in her pajamas. Yelling for my shoes as if they could hear me, Jackie knew something was wrong. I told her that Sarah called from Boston and said Jonathan had been shot. She asked who had told Auntie Sarah in Boston and why they didn't call us.

"Your Aunt Charlene!" I shouted.

I instructed Jackie to call the hospitals while I phoned the family or an Uber for a ride. I called or texted every family member I had in my cellphone for what seemed like an eternity. No one answered. All the calls went to voicemail. I then sent a group text and started calling again. It was close to 2 a.m., and I knew everyone was probably asleep. Hoping my son would answer, I called his cell again and reached his voice message.

"Boy, where are you? Pick up, call me back," was the message I left several times.

My next recourse was to call and wake up James to ask if he could pick me up and give me a ride to the hospital. After two attempts, he finally answered but said he was not home. I assumed he was out of state and told him never mind. What seemed like hours later, my cousin Kim called and said she and her brother-in-law were coming to pick me up. She did not explain, just told me to get dressed and hung up.

When she arrived at the house, I bolted out of the door, telling Jackie to keep calling the hospitals. She yelled back that the hospitals did not have anyone meeting Jonathan's description. That was impossible because we only had two hospitals in New Haven. Where else could he be? And Charlene was still not answering her phone.

While riding in the back seat of the car, no one spoke. I started complaining about the phone calls I had received from Boston informing me about my son. I was yelling that no family members were answering their calls all night. Turning my anger towards Kim, I asked her how she knew about all of this and why she had not come to pick me up sooner. Not allowing her time to respond, I continued to fuss. I told her that Jonathan should not have gone out, and I really hoped that he was alright.

Looking out the window, I wondered why we were not going in the direction of the hospital. I was confused. I could hear my cellphone phone ringing . . . "Ding . . . Ding . . . Ding . . . Ding . . . Ding." It kept making noise. I yelled at Kim, asking why we were not going in the direction of the hospital. Sitting in the front passenger seat, Kim snapped her head around and yelled at me.

"Put your cellphone down! Do not answer your cellphone and stay off social media. Promise me you won't even look at Facebook!"

I was shocked by Kim's harsh tone and anger. I am the one whose son was shot. What the heck was she mad about? I put my cellphone in my pocket and stared out the window, pouting and wondering where we were going.

I CAN'T TELL HER

It seemed like we had been driving for hours since we left my house. In reality, it had only been about 10 minutes when we arrived at the corner of Dixwell and Arch streets in Hamden. The streets were blocked off with yellow caution tape, and there were flashing lights from multiple police cars. The corner looked like a crime scene straight out of the "CSI Miami" television show. It was sheer chaos. Police officers were walking around, and my heart began racing. All I wanted to know was where was my son.

Kim started following me as I walked past all the cars parked in the middle of the street. I wondered who the people in these cars were and why they were here. It was then that I began to recognize my family members sitting in their cars, staring at all the police activity.

"Where is my son?" I yelled.

Glancing in and out of every car, no one opened their mouth. I spotted my car parked in the middle of the street with both front doors open.

As I walked through the crowd, my voice grew louder.

"Where is my son?"

Instead of answers, everyone kept saying, "Auntie, go ask Skeeter." Kim directed me toward the last car in the row. Everyone could hear the frustration and see the look of fear on my face. No one would answer my question. What was the big secret? My son must be here; I can see my car. I started yelling again.

"Skeeter, where is Jonathan?"

The passenger door of a car opened, and Skeeter emerged. As he opened the car door, the interior light came on, and I could see he was sitting in the car with Charlene, who turned her head away from the open door and remained in the car.

Skeeter dropped his head and said, "Auntie, Jonathan didn't make it."

I said, "I don't understand what you mean he didn't make it. He didn't make it where?" Skeeter then looked up and sadly said, "Jonathan was shot, Auntie; he's dead."

I stood frozen. I couldn't move my feet, couldn't move my body. I was standing there in unbelief. . . Unbelief. What did he say?

"Say it again," I said. "Did I hear you correctly? Did I hear you say that my son was dead?"

My knees buckled, crumbling beneath me. I fell, hitting the pavement with full force. I belted a cry of horror. The pain and hurt screeched out of my mouth. Kim grabbed me and pulled me into her arms.

My body shook in Kim's arm as she held me tighter. I can't believe this. It's not true. Somebody, please, please give me a different answer. It can't be true! Kim picked me up and held me, rocking me and telling me, "It's gonna be OK." But I pushed her away.

"Don't touch me! Nobody touch me! I don't want anybody to touch me! Don't come near me! All I want to know is where is my son. Where is my son?"

Running towards the yellow tape, I could hear people yelling, "Stop her! Someone grab Odell!"

I continued yelling, "Where's my son? I want to see my son!"

A police officer grabbed me and said, "Miss please, it's true, it's true. I can't let you go." He pinned me against the wall and confirmed that Skeeter identified my son, Jonathan Cooper's body, and he was dead. I demanded to see the body. The detective said no.

"Liars, liars! Where is my son?" I cried.

"Where is my son? Where is my son? I can't believe this. Where is my son?" I screamed.

A man kept picking me up from the pavement, but my legs kept collapsing. All I could say was, "Not my son, not my son! Where is my son?"

Onlookers stared at me with their mouths open in disbelief.

"What are you looking at me for?"

Then the truth became obvious? That's why they were there. Everybody knew the news before I did.

"Why didn't someone just tell me the truth?"

I no longer felt safe or secure. What other secrets were they keeping from me?

"No one is looking out for my best interest. I can't trust any of them. I need help," I thought.

Another detective approached and just stood there. He asked me something, but I couldn't hear him or understand his question. Everything people were saying sounded foreign. They were speaking a foreign language. This didn't make any sense. I just talked to my son, and he was fine.

Everyone knew Jonathan had been murdered, and no one told me the truth. Different thoughts were running through my head: What were they hiding or covering up? Was Skeeter near him when he died? I Wanted Answers!!

When the detective told me that Jonathan's body was still at the crime scene, I tried to run past the yellow tape. The detective stopped me and tightened his grip as I continued screaming in his arms. I needed to have someone around me I could trust. I felt alone and lost. I phoned James back and told him Jonathan had been murdered, and I needed him. He told me he was on his way. I thought he was in New York, and it would be a while before he arrived, so I called my director at ConnCAT and told him what happened. I asked him to come to the location; I needed help.

Still unable to get answers to what happened, I sat alone on the passenger floor in someone's car, sobbing uncontrollably. I was worried about how I was going to tell Jackie that her brother was dead.

The car door opened. It was my coworker. She pulled me to her, and she held me while I kept bawling in her arms. I stepped out of the car and noticed other coworkers were there with my director. James was also standing there. These Black men didn't know my family, and my family didn't know them. Therefore, anyone who wanted to come near me had to get through them. They would protect me. They would keep me safe and tell me the truth.

A detective walked over to me again and wanted to talk, but I couldn't speak. James asked where Jackie was and if she knew about Jonathan. I couldn't give her the bad news over the phone, so I pulled out my cellphone and called a deacon from my church. I managed to tell him I needed him to go to my house to be with Jackie because Jonathan had been murdered, and the police would probably show up. I needed somebody to take care of her until I got there.

We had all been together just 12 hours earlier, smiling and laughing with Jonathan, and now he was dead, and I didn't know why.

My phone rang in my pocket. It was the deacon calling to confirm that he was with Jackie at my house. Then I noticed the Facebook alerts. Someone had posted "Coop you will be missed" and tagged me in the pictures. My head pounded. I could barely read who was posting or what was being posted. All I saw was "RIP COOP."

I called his father before he heard or saw the news on social media. Why do people do this? Now I had to act fast. I cannot handle all this alone. When I reached his father, I gave him the dreadful news and told him to come immediately. I then called my son's sisters in New York. No one picked up, so I left a tearful, poorly articulated, panicky message asking them to call me ASAP. Then I tried to call his friends Marcel and Damar, but the calls went to voicemail. I could not leave a message, so I just hung up. I called back several times, hoping they would pick up. They needed to hear this news from me and not on social media.

My director managed to pull me away from the scene and drove me home. As we moved closer to my house, fear began swelling in my soul. How would I tell my daughter that her brother, her baby brother, born for her, was dead? When I saw Jackie, we both fell to the floor sobbing. I had to hold her. I needed her in my arms. How could I make her pain go away? There were no words to say, no hope to promise, no ministerial words of comfort for her soul. I just let her cry. When I finally looked up, I saw that Jackie wasn't alone. Her network of support had surrounded her. Tiffany looked at me with tears in her eyes and said, "Auntie, I came the moment my brother Skeeter called."

As a mother, I felt it was my responsibility to keep my children safe. How did I fail them? The rest of the night seemed like a blur. The sun began rising and peeked through the blinds. Stumbling upstairs to cry alone, I closed the door to my room and left Jackie alone.

I must have dozed off before I heard more voices downstairs. Voices were asking for me. When I opened my bedroom door and walked downstairs, Angel, Robin, and Sarah stood in my living room. How did they get here this fast? I never called them back with the truth. How did they know? What did they know? Apparently, Sarah knew my son had been murdered but could not tell me that news over the phone. She called my friends and told them the truth, which explained what I heard in Angel's voice. She, too, could not tell me the truth from another state. I didn't know how many tears I had left, but they kept coming. I wanted to wake up, and this be a dream, but more people walked through my door and called my phone, indicating this was not a dream.

Nonetheless, I kept thinking that this reality could not be possible. My son could not be dead. Everyone kept asking me, "What happened?" I didn't have an answer for them.

My house felt like a carousel for the next 36 hours. Church family, sorority sisters, friends, neighbors, coworkers were coming and going in rotations to share their condolences and disbelief. People kept coming!

It was exhausting. Everyone kept asking what I needed. At times I replied, "Bring my son back and let this all be a dream." They responded with looks of shock and fear, knowing that what I needed was not possible. At a loss for words, many just smiled and told me, "We will get through this." Eventually, I gave my phone to Angel to answer. I could not talk to another inquirer, another "well wishes," another "God will get you through this," another, "God needed an Angel," another, "God would not give you more than you can handle" phone call. The last call I accepted was from one of my sorority sisters telling me that she saw the news about Jonathan on Facebook. She was with a group at the Foxwood Casino, and they were all on their way to be with me. I didn't know who the "all" was, but before I could say, "Please stay and finish your retreat," she hung up.

I hated telling Jonathan's sisters over the phone, but the news was already on Facebook, and they heard the pain in my voice. It was now my responsibility to gain control and look presentable for Jackie. Someone forced me to go shower and change my clothes. I staggered to my bedroom to shower, obeying someone's order to "check out" for a while, and let them handle everything.

The warm water poured over my head as I cried. I did not want to move, praying that if I stayed in the shower, I would wake up, and this would be a dream. Someone knocked on the bathroom door, asking if I was alright. Then my reality started again.

I turned on the TV to drown out the noise downstairs. The

Saturday morning local news on Channel 8, WTNH, was on. The anchor said, "A 24-year-old Black man from Brooklyn, New York, was shot and killed at 1:30 am outside of Poppy's Pizza Bar in Hamden. His name has not been released until the family is notified." This news story hurt and made me angry because there was more to my son's story than reported.

A friend came to the house bogarting through everyone. She found me sitting and staring at the ceiling. Plopping down next to me, she grabbed my hand.

"God sent me to tell you that this did not come to break you," she said. "You can't be one of those mothers who never recover from this."

Looking into her face and holding back my tears, I said nothing. Inside, I was screaming, "Get the hell out of my house!!" She kept talking and praying for my future at a time when I felt disgusted and hopeless; the anger festered inside my soul. Eventually, she stopped talking and gave me a sisterly hug. Turning with her signature departure, "Sis', I got you," she left the house.

THE MORNING AFTER

The Boston crew left Sunday morning, promising to call me later and suggesting that I try to sleep. Although they were gone, the house was full of people. Later that day, Hamden Detective Onofrio arrived with additional questions. He walked in humbly and respectfully, politely acknowledging people he knew from the community and asked permission to talk with me. He didn't seem intimidated or confused by the mixture of clergy and community leaders in the house.

He expressed his sorrow for my son and asked if he could sit. Then he pulled out his notepad and began asking questions. It seemed that the information Jackie and I provided did not coincide with his investigative findings and he needed to review our answers again. He specifically wanted to know if Jonathan had been in Poppy's Pizza that night and if we knew of anyone who had a beef with him? Jackie jumped out of her chair and blurted out that her brother did not hang out at Poppy's.

"He spent the entire day with the family at ConnCAT, drove me to work, and had dinner with his mother until he went out with Skeeter. He had no reason to go inside that place; my brother did not run the streets."

I was startled by the rudeness and the tone of her voice, but she kept talking.

"My brother didn't live here, and people liked him," she said, in his defense.

The detective told us that a person with Jonathan that night gave conflicting stories about the timeline. Jackie was still irate and called them liars and wanted to know their names.

"My mother can prove it; she can track the car on her phone with the GPS and knows exactly where the car went that night."

The detective asked for my password and promised to recheck those stories further against my car's GPS and Jonathan's cellphone. He asked for the cell number and permission to review the phone records, promising to return the next day with a full explanation of Jonathan's whereabouts that evening. Jackie was still fussing to herself but loud enough for everyone in the house to hear.

"I don't understand what the problem is; it had to be mistaken identity," she fussed. "My mother's car has a Delta license plate and a Howard University Alumni bumper sticker. How could anyone mistake that car? My brother didn't hang out in that place. Whoever told you that lie, I will find out, and they will have to deal with me, lying on my brother."

Glancing up at the detective, I apologized for my daughter's tone but stressed we were all in shock. He continued with the questions on his pad. I confirmed Jonathan lived in Brooklyn, New York, and was a manager at Blue Stone Coffee Shop in Manhattan while attending music school there. He wanted to know why Jonathan moved to New York. I explained Jonathan enrolled in music school there and was working full time.

"Truthfully, detective, I didn't want my son living in New Haven for the same reason you are here today," I said. "These young Black men look and dress alike, and I wanted to keep him safe from these unnecessary shootings in New Haven. I guess it didn't work!"

THE BACK YARD

In the days after Jonathan's death, Jackie managed to take over the backyard with my son's friends. Before I retired to my bedroom one evening, one of my son's friends came inside, crying and wanting to talk to me.

"Momma Dukes, this didn't have to happen—should not have happened—to Coop. He was a good guy. It was not meant for him," he said. "I asked a few of my friends what they knew. It's been hard for me to tell you this, but it's only fair that you know."

He mentioned three men whose names were unfamiliar to me. As he kept talking through his tears and anger, he told me that these three men were at the pizza bar and had an argument with someone. They left and came back with guns. The person they were arguing with was gone. They saw Coop talking to someone in his car who might have been that person. They waited until Coop came out of the convenience store, followed him, and shot at the car. The bullets were not meant for Coop but someone else.

"I just wanted you to know, Momma Dukes, that it breaks my heart," he continued. "Coop didn't live here anymore, but everyone our age knows that place and that you do not go around that area on a Friday night at 1:30 in the morning.

"Everybody knows if you're not looking to get shot or score—I mean buy weed—you stay away from that corner! We're just all up-set that Coop ended up at that gas station at that time on Friday night because nobody goes there. Someone should have told him to go someplace else for cigarettes."

I was amazed this young man could answer my questions before the police department. Before leaving the room, he gave me a big hug.

"I am here if you and Jackie need anything," he said. "Also, I told Jackie who started the lie about Coop going to Poppy's that night, and she will talk to you later."

With every word, I pictured my son's last moments on earth. My eyes began watering, and tears started running down my cheeks.

"Momma Dukes, we love you," he said, dropping his head. "You have to know everyone in the backyard is so outraged. Coop did not deserve this. He didn't live here anymore, and everyone liked him."

I thanked him for the information and ran up to my bedroom. I fell on my bed, buried my head into my pillow, and pulled the blanket over my head to muffle my screams. At that moment, I was grateful that my bedroom resembled a loft; I could hide from everyone.

I stopped praying to wake up from a dream. Dreams don't last this long or have all these stories. This nightmare had to be real, and it was MY reality.

My bedroom window overlooked the deck and backyard. I had it cracked open to get some fresh air, hoping no one would hear my painful outburst. Instead, I got a whiff of the weed wafting through my bedroom window, and I knew they were also drinking by all the clinking bottles I heard. Every hour I overheard someone sharing a Coop story from grade school to adulthood. Some conversations I did not need to know. My son nicknamed me Momma Dukes, and somehow, that name entered the stories, and more laughter came. I was wondering how they could laugh at a time like this.

The firepit stories continued night after night in the backyard while I was inside lying in my bed, exhausted. I could not think of any fond memories of my son that would make me laugh. I wanted them to stop talking and go home. But I guessed it was their therapy.

I don't know how Marcel and Damar found out about Jonathan's death, but I heard their voices around the firepit as well. The group stayed outside from nightfall until 1 or 2 in the morning. Some mornings, I would find one of them passed out on Jackie's bed. I needed someone to help me regulate this crowd. I heard the pain and anger in their voices. They kept saying, "He didn't deserve this. Who did this to him?" Some even wanted revenge.

Days passed; I remained numb and confused. Someone came upstairs to tell me that two White ladies had arrived and were sitting at the table, refusing to leave until they saw me. Although barely awake, I went downstairs to greet my friends Liz and Checkbox. I sat with them and again had to retell the story and provide updates. They were there to offer support and assistance if I needed it.

On Monday, my ex-husband arrived from North Carolina. My niece moved her car so Michael could park his in my driveway. When she returned, she said, "Auntie, Uncle Mike is moving back home. If he has more than three bags, he's staying."

We all laughed, but I was getting nervous. My ex-husband came in with two bags and wanted to know where he was sleeping? I pointed to the family room that Coop had converted into his room. Michael went back outside and returned with two more bags and wireless speakers. My niece waited until he left the room and said, "Looks like Uncle Mike and Auntie are getting back together." Everyone laughed, but me.

WE GOT YOU

I needed some air, so I went to the local grocery store. While standing in line to check out, I heard the people standing in front of me discussing "the shooting that took place on the 23rd." The woman said, "What was he doing in Hamden at 1:30 a.m. if he lived in Brooklyn? Probably up to no good, buying drugs from Poppy's to take back to Brooklyn." The other woman agreed and said, "Where was his mother? He had no business being out at 1:30 in the morning."

I wanted to snatch them and say, "I am his mother, and my son wasn't buying drugs, and he had every right to be out!" I was so angry, but I knew that others had similar opinions. Driving home, I wondered why people were so judgmental of every Black man. Why couldn't their outlook be more optimistic instead of condemning? I am sure others stereotyped my son and prejudged him based on his age, gender, race, and reported circumstances.

Unfortunately, my son was one of many young Black men who had been shot or killed in that neighborhood within the past several months; that fact made me sick to my stomach. I had become immune to the past reports of young Black men being victims until now—until it was personal. The tears blurred my vision as I drove home. Fortunately, it seemed I was on autopilot.

Too often, the media has manipulated the narrative of our Black and Brown families, leaving us immune to the murders and twisted narratives. I wondered how I could change the narrative about my son. He did not deserve it. Then my head started thinking back to the news articles about Trayvon Martin, Eric Gardner and Mike Brown. No one would ever know my son's story because he was killed by another Black man and not the police. However, this didn't dismiss my anger or pain. We hear the news and shrug it off. Not this time; I needed to do something, but what? I possessed enough anger and rage to fight any system or people that suggested my son initiated his own murder by being a Black man and living free, by being in the wrong place at the wrong time to buy cigarettes.

When I returned home, I sat in the living room on the couch. I could not understand what was going on. I could not explain it, and I could not believe this was my life. How had this happened to me? What did I do? Could I have prevented it? Why did I let him go hang out with Skeeter in my car? It was my fault. I kept thinking if I had not changed the date of Friends and Family Day, my son would still be alive. I should have told him to pack his bags and to catch the train back to New York. Why did I ignore the voice? Was it the Holy Spirit speaking, and I ignored it? I could have saved his life! I could have said something that would have made a difference that night, but I did not.

Looking around the room, I saw food and bottles of alcohol. I saw guests mix Tito's Vodka and ginger ale, and they all seemed to enjoy it, so I made the same, hoping it would numb the pain and silence all the questions running through my head. Taking a huge, long sip, I shook to the taste and immediately felt the rush to my head. It was awful. I wondered why people drank this stuff. A few minutes later, I noticed my drink disappeared, and a cup of tea appeared in its place. I looked up to a warm smiling face that said, "Minister Cooper, drink this instead." Something told me not to argue with this woman who had a calm and pleasant smile.

"If you want to fight, I am prepared, been there and done that," she seemed to have said. So, I just smiled and drank the tea.

My granddaughter was too young to understand what was going on, but there were times she would walk up to me and say, "Nana, where's Uncle Coop? Is he coming back?" I couldn't find the words to respond to her. My voice was cracking, and I just said, "Uncle Coop is home. You will see him later." Thankfully, I did not have to worry about my granddaughter. Someone always made sure she had eaten, was bathed, and was safely in bed asleep.

Since Angel left, I gained possession of my cellphone, which kept ringing with dings from Facebook and text messages. Whenever I clicked on either, there were posts reading "RIP Coop," along with messages, photos, and videos. I wanted it to stop.

My cousin Norris came over and hugged me. I cried in his arms. He asked me what I needed. I asked that he stay with Michael and make sure the young people in the backyard cleaned up before they left and got home safely. He did that, taking off his cap and bringing a chair from the table, positioning it so he had a view of the back and front doors. His look said, "I am here to stay." Michael appreciated the company because I was not sociable, and we never talked about losing our son. I never saw him cry. He came in the house and re-sumed his old role of being in charge.

Finally able to return to my room and try to sleep, I could hear Michael and Norris at the table laughing and reminiscing about the early years when he and I were married, and the two of them were hanging out. Between the marriage memories emanating from the dining room and Coop stories at the backyard firepit, the house was full of people, love, memories, laughter, and tears. About midnight, I heard Michael and Norris tell everyone in the backyard that it was time to leave. They did not respond, and then I heard, "Jackie, your mother said everyone needs to go home. You all do not want her to come downstairs." Really? Why did they have to blame me? I heard the grumbling voices from the backyard, but they left.

Hours later, the house was quiet. For once, I was relieved of the responsibility of securing the house and making sure everyone was safe. This responsibility was exhausting. I was able to doze off until the sun came peering through my skylight. It was morning, and it was time to repeat yesterday. The day began and ended the same way.

That night, I had enough. I told Jackie and Michael that we are shutting down the house tomorrow, no company, no firepit, no one.

"Put a sign on the door that says, 'We need to be alone, please respect our privacy,'" I said.

We needed time as a family to embrace and cry together. Michael and I sat on either end of the couch, with Jackie in the middle. We held each other and cried. I am not sure how long it lasted, but I was awakened by the sun again, creeping through my skylight the following day.

❋

My son's murder did not stop the family from creating conflict and confusion. The lies and false stories about my son's whereabouts that night began traveling via text messages or phone calls throughout the family. Aggravated with the nonsense, I phoned my nieces Nichelle and Tanya, who were living in Maryland and were planning to arrive on the day of the service, which at that point was five days away. Because he was murdered, the coroner had not released the body. I asked Nichelle and Tanya if they could come sooner. Without repeating the details of the family drama, they both understood my request. Nichelle admitted she heard some of the drama and wondered how I was dealing with it. During the phone call, they both promised to arrive by the next night. Before hanging up, Nichelle said, "We Got You!"

My director stopped by my house later that day to check on us and find out about Jonathan's service. He told me to take as much time off from work as I needed. I thanked him and told him about the Channel 8 News story that I thought unfairly reported my son's murder. He gave me the contact information of a Black reporter at the New Haven Register—Shahid Abdul-Karim—and suggested I contact him to re-write the narrative. I called Mr. Abdul-Karim, and he graciously agreed to write the article. We set a date to meet after Jonathan's homegoing service.

Cousins from Florida and friends from Texas called and confirmed their arrival. Although I told them they did not need to make the long journey for Jonathan's service, they assured me they were coming, saying simply, "We got you."

After Nichelle, Tanya and JoAnn (their mom and my sister) arrived as promised, I relinquished the household to them and went upstairs to sleep. Anything that happened or needed to happen had to get their approval. My house looked and smelled like a flower shop. Plants and flowers were positioned anywhere in the living room, bathroom, dining room, and my office where there was space. Sympathy cards were standing everywhere until Nichelle and Tanya started a folder with envelopes so I could send thank you cards.

The love and affection were overwhelming. Nichelle sat on the living room couch next to the open front door—thankfully, it was a warm April—most of the day greeting people and signing for whatever was delivered.

Jackie and I agreed we did not want to see Jonathan in a casket and decided to have him cremated. However, we needed the approval of his father and siblings. Everyone approved.

Because Jonathan's remains were not released, we did not have a death certificate. Without a death certificate, I could not receive the insurance money for the service. The funeral director suggested the Office of Victim Services might help us. When someone is murdered without fault, the state offered monies to cover funeral services and other support. Thankfully, the funeral director volunteered to handle all the paperwork, only requiring my signature to move forward with seeking help from the Office of Victim Services.

I insisted on writing my son's obituary, but my sorors hovered, correcting all the mistakes. They edited my words through my tears. In hindsight, I think someone should have just pushed me out of the chair and taken over. My decision to write Jonathan's obituary was not smart.

Brenda Lammie, Jonathan's godmother, made a collage of beautiful photos for the service.

I had a new appreciation for the families who sat in the front pew of the church when they had to bury a murdered son. How is anyone expected to handle this number of details and remain untraumatized?

MENDING BROKEN RELATIONSHIPS

I received a call from Michael's twin daughters Margarette and Arynce telling me they were coming to the house. I told them their father was in town and staying at the house. They had not seen or spoken to him in over 30 years, since the day they came to Connecticut and met us for the first time. Now, they were face-to-face with their father for the second time in their lives. The resemblance was striking. All of Michael's children had chocolate skin, his strong nose, full lips, and were tall and slim like him. Jonathan would have been proud of this moment. He was all about family. It was sad that he was absent. Michael had an older son who also lived in New York but was not present. At one point, I had arranged for all five siblings to meet for the first time with the mothers. All three of us ranged drastically in height and skin complexion. We took several photos during that meeting. I had no idea what we all had in common other than being women. However, Michael told me that both mothers ended the relationship with him as if he was not at fault.

Once the twins arrived at my house, they lingered outside for 30 minutes before coming inside. Finally, they both walked through the door and acted as if Michael was not in the room. You could feel the anger, tension and resentment in the air. However, we needed to discuss the funeral services as a family. I had two requests: In lieu of flowers, we asked donations to be made to the Mount Aery Church Media Ministry in which Jonathan was actively involved; and I asked my pastor to keep the service to an hour. Everyone agreed and fortunately, through the planning, the tension broke, and the twins began speaking directly to Michael. Michael was equally emotional during his daughters' visit but tried to disguise his feelings. He later thanked me for keeping in touch with his daughters.

There were so many calls, messages, visits, and acts of kindness from all those who knew Jonathan. I received a Facebook message from a woman in New York telling me about her interactions with

Jonathan and that she enjoyed his playlist of music. I was shocked because I never liked his music, but I thanked her. Feeling all of the love made me proud of the man my son had become. At the same time, I was angry because his life ended too soon. My son was gone! I wondered if Jonathan knew how people perceived him as a respectful young Black man.

The funeral director kept his promise and arranged for the family to view the body before the homegoing service. Jonathan's body was wrapped in a cloth but still in the black body bag. The assistant would not let us touch his face, being very protective of that area of his body. I don't know how the undertaker managed to maintain the infamous smile on his face. My son had his smile. The viewing was difficult and surreal. I didn't want to leave my son; leaving meant I would never see him again.

Jackie was still trying to be strong for me, but the tears poured down her face, and her glasses were foggy. Our hearts were crushed. Losing our Jonathan was not fair and senseless. How do you say goodbye to your son, who shouldn't be lying in a black body bag with a blanket covering his neck? Jackie was saying goodbye to her best friend, her brother. We stayed a little under an hour before leaving, and we drove home in silence. I looked at Michael; he was still trying to be strong for us, but this was his son. We were saying goodbye to our son.

The next day was the service, and the house was full of family sleeping everywhere. While I was making a plate from all the food in the house, Michael came upstairs to inform me that the water heater broke, leaving an inch of water in the family room where Michael had been staying. He managed to turn off the water and retrieve Jonathan's clothing from being destroyed. So, in addition to saying goodbye to my son the next day, I had to secure a plumber and purchase a new water heater immediately. Placing my grief aside, Angel drove me to the store at 7 a.m. I was able to hire a plumber on a Saturday, and before we left for the church, the house was back to normal; we had hot water.

THE FRONT PEW

I dreaded walking into the church for this moment in my life. My role as associate minister at Mount Aery was to console the families sitting in the front pew. Now, I had to sit in the pew and let the other ministers comfort my family and me. It was painful.

I hoped Pastor Bennett remembered my request to keep the service to an hour. I wanted to leave. When the family lined up for the processional into the church, I saw two unexpected guests at the door. Gail and Maria were two women I had not seen since we graduated from high school in 1980. I walked down the stairs and greeted them with gratitude and appreciation.

As we were walking into the church, my granddaughter looked at me and said, "Nana is Uncle Coop going to be here?" I finally had to tell her that Uncle Coop was in heaven. I would do my best to keep the memory of my son, her Uncle Coop, alive in her memory. I would keep his pictures so that she could never, ever forget him. She would never forget how much he loved her, how much he loved being called Uncle Coop. I wanted her to remember how special and loved she was.

There was not an empty seat in the 700-seat capacity sanctuary. For the first time, I didn't have to concern myself with making sure the family was seated. I didn't want to be seated; anyone could have my pew. Sitting in the front pew on a day like today meant someone died, and the closer you sat to the pulpit defined your relationship to the deceased. Not me, please God, not me. I don't want to sit in the front pew. I wanted to be anywhere but where I was. As I inched closer to the first row, my heart ached, and the reality of this nightmare seemed more surreal. The ministers I had trained over the years from BMP were making their way toward the pulpit. And Rev. Watts, who was now bishop, was seated in the pulpit. The ushers, deacons, and my church family were present and standing alongside the walls in the sanctuary.

Jackie sat between her father and me. We were saying goodbye to the family member who kept all of us smiling, our bridge, my son. We had to say goodbye to the one who helped us solve our differences and arguments. The glue was gone.

Jackie proudly stood between her sisters and shared a lovely story about her little brother.

"I raised him, dressed him, and taught him everything he knew," she said. Her words almost sounded like a mother saying goodbye to her child. I had to wonder if she did all that, what did I do? I was proud and scared at the same time.

Jonathan would often return to our home church, Varick AME Zion Church, with Marcel and enjoyed the preaching and relationship with the pastor, who gave the prayer of comfort. On such a sad day, I was warmed to have my extended church family supporting us. It must have been difficult for them, too, as Jonathan grew up there.

Pastor Bennett asked permission to preach a little longer.

"Odell asked that I keep the service to an hour, but I am standing here witnessing how wide and diverse the community of support is for the Cooper family, and I want to honor this time of love," he said.

Pastor asked Michael and me to stand and view the diversity in the room—ages, professions, ethnicities, genders. I was both honored and sad. He thanked all those present who supported us.

When the service ended, I made my way downstairs to the repast and made my rounds to thank all those present on this sad day. I looked up and saw Alonzo, and I was glad he was able to be present. Without speaking, he knew my pain. He and Jonathan had enjoyed talking basketball and life. Michael took a family picture that included the twins and their husbands and their mother—a picture that took 36 years to create.

The younger friends and families of Jackie and Jonathan had difficulty attending the repast. Marcel and Damar were not present. Both were still hurt and angry and wanted answers.

I was grateful for the love and support of my Mount Aery church family. After the repast, Michael and I drove back to my house to greet more people who came by to share their condolences.

Michael noticed that Tony and James were present at the house.

He pulled me aside and apologized for being jealous of my male friends, church friends and sorority sisters. Michael explained that he had wanted me to stay home and be with him. He now realized all the others in my life were true friends who cared about me. I wanted to reach up and smack him in the face. His apology was more hurtful than comforting. I lost a child for no logical reason, and now my ex-husband was saying that our divorce resulted from the same thing, stupidity.

Standing in my living room, a group of women I had never seen before approached me. One of them handed me a card and introduced the group as Mothers of Homicide. I turned my back, crouching in pain. I cried out. This was a club I didn't apply for membership in and didn't want to need them. I wanted my life back where I prayed for them and gave their group support and encouragement. The reality was like a slap in the face. I was now a mother whose child had been murdered and a member of Mothers of Homicide, Survivors of Homicide, and any other grieving mothers' group in the state and country. The women knew my pain and understood the journey I was now traveling. They left a flyer for me, and I heard them ask someone in the room to have me call when I was ready. The pain and anger were cutting deeper into my heart. When does this stop? When does God stop slapping me in the face with this unbearable pain and reality? Where are you God, this is more than I can bear.

Throughout the afternoon, others came to hug me and give me words of comfort. The pastor from Christian Tabernacle Church in Hamden came by to pay his respects. We had been friends since Howard University. The pastor once told my children if they ever found themselves in trouble, he was their lawyer. They took that comment to heart and always knew the pastor meant what he said.

CHANGING THE MEDIA NARRATIVE

Monday morning, Shahid Abdul-Karim, editor for the New Haven Register, kept his promise and came to interview our family, allowing us to tell the truth about Jonathan Michael Cooper. The truth was he was an innocent 24-year-old Black man who was born, educated, and worked in Connecticut only to be wrongfully murdered. Karim allowed us to rewrite the negative narrative and perception of my son's murder. Karim reiterated that people probably wouldn't read it, nor would it make a difference, but it supported our attempt to change the narrative of the innocent, young Black men murdered. When he left the house, the anger and fight still burned at the core of my soul and did not subside.

Everyone returned to their homes, and the quiet was airy. I did not have a car, keys to my house, nor the energy to rationalize what I needed to do next. Still wearing my boxing gloves, I was ready to fight another cause, system, or person to release my anger.

Jackie decided to return to school and her part-time job at a gourmet grocery store in downtown New Haven. Much to our surprise, the New Haven Register printed the article about Jonathan on the front page on Monday, May 2, 2016. Later that evening, Jackie bolted through the front door with tears in her eyes.

"I quit! I can't do this anymore!" she said. "I asked you to stop, and you keep doing it! I go to work to try to keep my mind off of losing my brother, but every time I turn around, somebody is walking up to me offering their condolences because they saw my picture on the front page of the New Haven Register. They are constantly reminding me that my brother is dead.

"Mom, I know you mean well. I know you're trying to correct the wrong, but you can't fight everybody. You're not thinking about me; you're not considering my feelings. So please stop!"

I HAVE PTSD

Jackie wanted to go to school, raise her daughter, and work through healing on her own without talking. Although we lived in the same house, we barely spoke to one another. She ate in her room while watching television or spending time with her daughter. I came into the house and went straight to my room. Our only conversation was about bills and my schedule for her daughter. Jackie had been posting her feelings, thoughts, and emotions on Facebook and receiving words of healing via social media. I did not agree with this method of healing, but she politely reminded me that people her age don't seek counseling and that she was fine.

My director approved my request for an additional week off to heal.

"Take your time, no rush," he said.

I did not know what that meant. I needed my job and money to pay bills. I had no idea what to do next. I staggered upstairs to a to-do list on my dresser that was signed, "Love Nichelle and Tanya." I had no idea what was ahead for Jackie and me without Jonathan in our lives.

As I thought about life without my son, a chill ran down my spine, causing me to shiver uncontrollably. My thoughts raced back to the crime scene and the clusters of family members who huddled in their little groups, not talking to me. I continued to worry and agonize about why it was taking the detectives so long to find the person or persons responsible for my son's murder. The conversation his friend and I had regarding that night came to mind, and it occurred to me the police still hadn't provided an update. The ringing doorbell snapped me out of my daze. Coincidentally, it was the detective at the door with an update on his investigation. Jackie joined us in the living room, and we listened carefully.

Based on information gathered from the GPS and text messages from Jonathan's phone, according to the detective, this is what happened:

Jonathan drove to the gas station across the street from Poppy's to purchase cigarettes. Skeeter was sitting in the passenger side with the seat pushed back and you could not see him. Video camera recordings from the area show Jonathan getting into the car and taking a right turn out of the parking lot, instead of a left, which was the direction back to house. He asked, "why would Jonathan drive in the opposite direction if he was only taking Skeeter to get cigarettes before returning home?" We didn't have an answer, so he kept talking. The camera shows a car hurrying out of Poppy's parking lot and the driver looking at Jonathan across the street. The car pulled out and followed them to the traffic light. The car pulled up alongside them. There were three young men in the car and shots were fired.

I stopped the detective from talking because I could not bear to hear any more about my son's death. Taking a deep breath and exhaling, the detective continued.

"It appears your son was unaware that he was followed and in danger," he said. "Skeeter saw your son was shot, jumped out of the car, and ran across the street for help. By the time he returned with help, Jonathan was dead.

"Your son was the victim of mistaken identity," he continued. "Jonathan didn't live in New Haven anymore. He was not aware people avoid that area on Friday nights due to the high level of crime and shootings on that corner."

What the detective was telling us was difficult to hear—the senselessness of it all.

"Everyone we asked about your son had only good things to say about him," he said. "Jonathan was never associated with gangs. He was a good young man by all reports."

Irritated, Jackie responded in a sharp tone. "I told you that three weeks ago! I already knew that. I knew it had to be a mistake. My brother was a good person. He didn't deserve to die like that!"

She stormed out of the room.

I told the detective that I was upset the police spent more time investigating my son's character than his case. He apologized for the longer investigation but reiterated people who were with Jonathan that night gave false statements.

"Once we tracked the GPS and reviewed everyone's text messages, we were able to have an accurate timeline of what really happened that night," he said.

We told detectives weeks ago about Jonathan's character. It hurt like hell knowing my son died alone on Dixwell Avenue, bleeding to death. My eyes filled with tears thinking about Jonathan's last thoughts.

"Unfortunately, your son was one of many young Black men who have been shot or killed in that neighborhood within the past several months," he said, as he apologized for the painful investigative process. "Your son's case is unique in many ways but being a victim of gun violence in that neighborhood is not one of them. Many of these crimes have commonalities: The location and time of day were the most glaring similarities with Jonathan's case.

"Poppy's had been a constant problem, with the neighbors living in constant fear of gunfire and violence. It has created victims and destroyed families."

After telling me he would keep us posted on anything further in the investigation, the detective left the house and us alone with our growing anger.

The following morning, a ConnCAT board member called to check on my welfare and asked me to meet him at a local breakfast spot on State Street. It was a small, quaint restaurant with limited seating. Arriving with an appetite for a small stack of blueberry pancakes and bacon, I hadn't realized how hungry I was. Unfortunately, the restaurant only served a variety of coffees and muffins. I adjusted my nose to inhale the scent of vanilla bean coffee, which was a pleasant alternative. Based on the menu options, I thought that this would be a quick check-in.

As soon as we sat down, the board member shared his story about being a veteran and told me about his time in the service. He discussed suffering from Post-Traumatic Stress Disorder (PTSD) and bouts of depression, which affected his personal and professional life. He described his feelings of anger and confusion, and how he coped with these conditions. I was confused as to why he was telling me this story. Immediately, I assumed the role of Minister Cooper, and shared words of comfort. He blankly stared at me as if I were missing the point of his story. Not understanding his reaction, I thanked him for speaking with me and left to find pancakes elsewhere.

Earlier that morning, Jackie returned to culinary school, so I was home alone. I needed to figure out how to tackle the to-do-list

Nichelle and Tanya left on my dresser. First on the list was to replace my car. For the first time since I moved to Connecticut, I caught the bus, and went to the Mazda dealership in Hamden. I had been a faithful customer at the dealership for the last 10 years, and I was hopeful the manager could solve my car issue. As I approached the lobby, I saw the manager, who was my sorority sister's husband. He knew about my son's murder, so I did not believe I had to reshare my trauma.

He suggested I grab lunch and come back in two hours. When I returned, I had been approved to lease a new car, pending the paperwork from the insurance adjuster. He worked a miracle! I selected a different make, model, and color car. Thankfully, I was promised the car by the end of the week. I left feeling a sigh of relief.

CHAPTER 10
INTERRUPTION: ASK ME ANOTHER QUESTION

RETURNING HOME, I SAT IN MY front yard in my blue Adirondack chair underneath my tree. I needed time to exhale before walking into the house and facing my reality. Inside, my house smelled like a florist shop and looked like the center aisle of the CVS greeting card section.

As I sat outside, I reminisced about my son learning to cut the grass for the first time. He was barely 3-feet tall, and 100 lbs. His head barely reached the lawnmower handles. I would watch him peek through the handles for directions from me as he pushed the lawnmower. The grass was cut crooked, but it was cut. There was not a straight line in the front yard. As he grew taller, his gardening skills improved.

The ringing cellphone broke my daydreaming. Another friend was calling to ask how I was feeling? Taking a deep breath, I decided to speak my truth. I was numb before when these calls came through, not anymore. My tone of voice changed; it grew deeper. Soon the words came spewing out my mouth.

"How do you think I feel?" I snapped. "My son was murdered! Someone ripped my heart out of my chest and turned my life upside down. I cannot sleep, eat, and truthfully, I am mad at God for not saving my son. So, the answer to your question is, ask me another question."

The person on the other end must have been shocked at my response. The phone went silent, so I hung up. Minutes later, another person called with a similar question, and I replied, "Horrible!" She responded, "That's good, you know you are a strong Black woman, and God has you." Obviously, she didn't hear anything I said. Again, I responded, "Ask me another question." I could hear her breathing, but she did not speak, so I hung up.

The calls kept coming, with the callers asking the same well-meaning but useless question. I soon realized some people did not listen or realize that their questions and comments were clichés and more painful than comforting. I knew they were calling with good intentions, but the calls were not supportive. Call after call, all I heard were statements such as "God needed another angel;" "Where God guides, God provides;" "If God brings you to it, He will bring you through it;" "Man meant it for evil, but God meant it for good;" and the worst was "And Jesus says . . ."

I wasn't in the mood to hear the goodness of Jesus. My son was murdered. The anger and pain mounted deeper inside my soul with every phone call or text. In what seemed like the 100th call, this caller quoted scripture, suggesting I read the book of Job in the Old Testament of the Bible.

"Job lost his family and never cursed God and was blessed," the caller said.

Now I was insulted. Did she even know who I was? A minister at Mount Aery Baptist Church and a seminary graduate—and she was telling me to read the book of Job. I told the caller that I wasn't cursing God but was just mad. The caller began to lecture me about being a Christian, admonishing me that as a minister of the church, I should not question God. I thanked her for calling and hung up.

I was mad at God for not saving my son. I believed that God and I had a relationship. I worked and taught for God, studied and strived to be obedient to the scriptures and Christian values. I had the right to ask God a question. However, I knew the importance of not hardening my heart because God would not bless me. I was mad, not stupid. My anger was with God because He gave Satan permission to let my son die. The pain of losing my son had created this hostile attitude toward my God and faith. As a Christian, I believed in the Apostles Creed, the concept of the Trinity—God the Father, God the

Son, and God the Holy Spirit. In the Christian bible, Jesus teaches us how to pray. Nana always said to approach God with reverence and a calm, patient spirit. My son was murdered, and I couldn't find the neat and appropriate scriptures to talk with my God.

God knew that every fiber of my being was torn to shreds. I had to tell my daughter that I could not keep her brother safe. In her eyes, her brother was born for her, so she wouldn't be alone and would be less annoying. If my God is all-knowing, then He knew how much pain I was feeling. It wasn't about a neat and pleasant conversation. This time, our relationship was messy, so messy that my ability to quote scripture to get His attention was not happening. God knew my relationship with Him and my heart and was expecting this behavior from me. Our relationship was now messy. My conversation was straightforward, and all the formalities and proper etiquette of communication were gone.

I remembered reading the scripture that said, "Evening and morning and at noon I utter my complaint and moan, and he hears my voice." Anyone who dared to enter my space needed to be prepared to deal with my pain and hostile attitude. I was not apologetic.

JEHOVAH'S WITNESS

Once again, the following day, I found myself sitting in the same chair in my front yard, daydreaming, trying to escape my reality when I noticed a car pull in front of my house. I didn't recognize the driver. A woman parked and got out of the car smiling and walked towards me. I could tell she was a Jehovah's Witness based on her dress and how she was carrying the bible. She was coming to talk about God. I did not want to be mean, but I was not in the mood. She had a pleasant smile and demeanor and asked if she could sit down and talk. I motioned to the second chair underneath the tree. She introduced herself and sat down.

"I am glad to finally catch you home relaxing," she said. "How are you feeling today?"

This last question was her mistake. She presumed something was wrong based on my teary eyes and clenched teeth. She reached for her bible and wanted to read a scripture. I abruptly stopped her.

"I don't want to hear that God saves, and He never gives us more than we can handle," I said.

Appearing shocked and unsure how to respond, she didn't expect my response. She began to quote a scripture without looking at her bible. I completed the scripture and gave her an evil look. She asked if she could leave me The Watchtower.

"Read the pamphlet. It will bring you comfort to read about the good news of God," she said.

Feeling numb, fighting back tears, and trying my best to keep the painful words from spewing from my lips, I took the pamphlet and said thank you. She stood up and continued to give me a warm smile. When she asked if she could return another day, I stared at her with tears flowing from my eyes and asked her to keep driving past my house tomorrow.

"Don't worry about stopping here. I have nothing to offer but painful conversation."

I didn't enjoy being rude and disrespectful. Doing so was out of character for me. I couldn't explain my rage. I was not acting like myself.

"Miss Odell, I will keep you in prayer and return next week to check in on you," she politely replied.

TRIGGERS

I returned to work at the culinary school the following Monday. I looked the same on the outside but wasn't sleeping and felt mentally exhausted. It was a struggle to get out of bed. I wore my son's red, wireless Beats headset around my neck. It was my way of keeping him close to me. The moment I walked into the lobby, I envisioned Jonathan standing there saying, "Mom, are you ready to leave?" Holding back the instant pain I felt, I pushed my way to my office for a moment of privacy and began sobbing. I had no idea if I could complete the day.

Jackie came into my office to say good morning. Even though we lived in the same house, we still didn't see each other. I was just glad to know she was out of the house working. Jackie's smile seemed forced, but she was in her culinary whites. She told me that the students were glad that I was back. On a more personal note, she advised me to take it easy, don't overdo, and if I needed anything to let her know. She also asked whether I could pick Maya up from school.

I had always enjoyed my position as director of the culinary program. However, now I did not feel like the same person. Entering the building where my son once worked as a security officer and spent his last day at my request was challenging. During the day, I forgot appointments and seemed unable to complete tasks without crying. While attending meetings, someone would innocently say something that triggered an erratic emotion or an inappropriate response from me. I found myself present at the meetings but not attentive or coherent. I was causing conflict and confusion. I was given assignments and immediately would forget the conversation ever happened. I would leave a meeting, return to my office, and send incorrect emails. It appeared my director was coming into my office more frequently, seeking an explanation for my work behavior. I could not defend or explain my actions because I wasn't aware of the mistakes, leaving the impression that I was dishonest and not accountable for my actions. These were behaviors contrary to my work ethic. My director often left the room more confused and perplexed than when he entered. This scenario continued for months. I knew something had to change soon, but just didn't know what.

Walking out of my office into the culinary kitchen, I saw a vision of Jonathan standing next to the table smiling. The image triggered another negative emotion. Shaking off the vision, I realized that it was another student, who was asking me a question. I turned around and bolted back to my office. My inconsistent responses were becoming a regular occurrence, and I began to feel the increased tension at work. Many days my coworkers walked into my office and found me crying uncontrollably. I always said I was OK, but inside, I was in pain. There were days I stayed late to correct my errors, but it was difficult to concentrate on a single task without forgetting what I was doing.

After leaving work, I usually picked up my granddaughter from daycare. The staff was always warm and supportive. They stopped asking me how I was feeling or doing. Instead, they just greeted me with a smile and hug. I packed my granddaughter in the car and drove home in silence. Maya was accustomed to us playing music in the car, talking about her day, and discussing what she wanted for dinner. Every Friday night, she and I would have a pajama party, listen to music and dance to her favorite videos, drink hot tea and blue chips and salsa. Some nights were a special treat. We would eat smoked gouda cheese and crackers.

I would pull out the futon bed and grab her stuffed animals. We said our prayers, and she fell asleep. That had been our routine for the last year. But now things had changed, and I couldn't explain my emotions or behavior. As soon as my daughter walked through the door from work, we briefly greeted each other, then I walked up the stairs to my room. I could feel my knees beginning to collapse with every step. Would I make it or fall in the middle of the staircase and sob myself asleep? My granddaughter would ask if she could sleep upstairs and drink tea. I turned around and saw her little eyes looking up at me. I did not respond. Not responding was my way of again saying, "not tonight."

In my room, I slid to my knees onto Jonathan's futon, sobbing. I asked God "Where is my son? Why didn't you save him?" I told God He could do anything and save anyone. He had all powers in His hands. So why didn't He save my son? Eventually, I fell asleep on my knees crying. The next morning, I struggled to get out of bed, but returned to work, and by noon I was mentally exhausted. All my efforts to correct the previous day's mistakes were futile. I was missing my son. Trying to mask the pain and anger was not working.

One night a friend met me at my house, and we went to a neighborhood restaurant for dinner. Usually, we sat at tables either in the back or on the side. This time I didn't care and grabbed a seat at the bar. I knew most of the people there because it was a place that I frequented. People were surprised to see me out, appearing to enjoy myself, and they bought our drinks. I'm not a drinker. Usually I ordered a glass of wine, but on this evening, my behavior was different. I had a hole to fill, and maybe the alcohol would help. Unable to consume all the free drinks, I shared them with others. By the time I left the bar, the pain seemed to be gone. I was laughing and joking for the first time in months. I needed this kind of night out. However, that one night turned into three weeks with someone different, sitting at the bar and drinking, trying to fill the hole in my soul, and it wasn't working.

Every morning, my head would spin, and the pain of losing my son returned. Work became a blur. I looked forward to the time I left work to pick up my granddaughter and then later sit at the bar. One night, I rummaged through my medicine cabinet, trying to find something to take and never wake up. All I had was Tylenol—not even Tylenol PM. Again, I went to the futon, dropped to my knees, and began crying to God with the same questions. The pain was too heavy to carry. All I could think about were ways to remove this pain.

That following day, my friend Checkbox came to my office. I had stopped answering her phone calls and texts. We sat in my office talking, and she suggested I make an appointment to see a trauma counselor. What was a trauma counselor, and why did I need to see one? She reminded me that a mutual acquaintance was a trauma counselor. Checkbox began describing my feelings as if she was in the room with me. She described triggers, and all the other emotions I was experiencing, which meant I needed counseling. I wondered how she knew all these things about me. I didn't realize my behavior had changed that much. We talked about different types of medication, and Checkbox suggested I ask the counselor for something to assist me in sleeping through the night. She promised I would feel better in the morning. To get Checkbox to stop talking and leave my office, I made the appointment that day.

The Jehovah's Witness returned to my home. I could not understand why she kept returning for the same abuse. I didn't read the pamphlet she left, so she began reading the scriptures to me instead. I reluctantly listened and didn't interrupt her process. She departed with the same hopeful and promising smile.

Sunday morning, I returned to church. During the service, all I could do was worship God from the floor. I was too emotional and weak to stand. I fell to my knees, and the Pastor's wife came to support me. She didn't pick me up or quote scriptures or ask one of the male deacons to escort me to the quiet room away from the sanctuary. Instead, she sat on the church floor with me and held me in her arms while I sobbed through the entire church service. As I worshipped from the floor, Pastor Bennett continued preaching and allowed me to be. After service ended, some members stopped to speak to me.

"Minister Cooper, God told me to tell you that . . .," one member felt the need to say.

I stopped her before she could finish and told her, "God and I have a relationship, and He will tell me what I need to know."

Another member reminded me that I was strong and told me to have hope.

"God loves you," she said. "He never gives you more than you can handle."

I responded, that was an untrue statement and she should read the bible again.

Although the member's clichés were well-intentioned, they were not comforting nor promising. I wanted to give her a quick biblical lesson on the scripture, but my tone of voice would have been angry. My son's death and all these Christian clichés were more than I could bear. However, I knew it would not always be this painful, but this was my life now and what I had to endure.

A member of the grief ministry stopped and asked if she and others in the ministry could come by the house and pray with me?

"No. I am not grieving," I told her. "I am traumatized."

My response was not what she expected, and I could tell she was disappointed. But what I loved most were the senior saints of the church who could relate to my anguish. They would walk up to me and wrap their arms of comfort around me. I could feel the unspoken message, "I've been there, sweetie, and here is the love you need to keep you strong."

One of the church members, Nurse Betty, and I have a special relationship. When I first joined the church, she occasionally pulled me to the side and provided a correction or compliment. Always watching me from the corner of her eye, she was direct and forthcoming about how a new minister in the church should conduct herself. I always listened and didn't argue. On this day, she quietly sat in a chair. Once the crowd dissipated, she told me to go directly home, don't open Facebook, or answer the phone. She scheduled a meeting with me for the following week to provide me with a Reiki therapy, an alternative medicine practice.

After the session, she was concerned about not being able to move the energy from my head. Nurse Betty insisted that I relax more or meditate.

Sunday night came without change. I slept in my bed and had a horrible nightmare; I woke up scared and crying. The dream was dark and riddled with evil temptations. It seemed real, as if I were physically present. I wondered why I was still alive and how I could end this pain I was carrying in my heart. These moments were depressing. For the next few nights, the nightmare continued. I was now afraid to sleep in my bed. I stood in the middle of my room, traumatized by the thought of going to sleep, staring at the bed, afraid.

Another month passed, but the pain did not subside. I was miserable at work, wanting only to sleep. I stopped talking to everyone. When my friends from Boston called, my response was the same: "Ask me another question." They could hear something was different in my voice and strongly suggested I see a counselor. God blessed me with an all-star, dream praying team. They made themselves available 24/7. Whenever I called, they prayed me out of bed, through the day, to sleep and strength through the nightmares.

During calls I occasionally posed questions to these prayer warriors.

"Tell me something you believe about God, but you couldn't teach in school or share from the pulpit. Something about God that was not in the scriptures, but you believe in your heart."

I needed to understand God in a way that I had not been taught before.

One team member responded with a story that ended in, "God saves souls." I was struggling with why God let my son die. Why did he not save his life?

Rev. Anderson solicited the assistance of another associate minister for additional support, and Brenda Lammie met with me every Tuesday. We did not have a planned agenda. She was just present and able to deal with my depressive mood swings.

My praying dream team members made themselves available to me during the first year after Jonathan died. Their availability and prayers made a difference in my life. One night, I begged God to accompany me into my dreams. Falling asleep crying and scared had become my new normal. Satan had been tormenting me for weeks. I was tired of being defeated. I didn't understand what was going on. I was too weak and unable to fight this battle. I knew if I succumbed to these evil temptations, there would be no turning around. Satan would steal my soul. He was familiar with people and loved to offer evil seductions.

Once, while sleeping, I touched the hand of someone offering me something evil. Their face changed to a dark skeleton. I could not win this battle. I cautiously crawled into my bed and began praying and petitioning God to go before me and stay with me while I slept. I was asking God to step out from His throne and keep His promise. God promised at least 400 and 14 times from the book of Genesis to the Christmas account that Jesus would show up and crush the head of Satan and he would not win. My alarm rang at six a.m., and I realized the nightmares were over. I felt refreshed for the first time in weeks. I said out loud, "In the name of Jesus, thank you!" I was ready to start another day.

BACK TO THE NEIGHBORHOOD

Jackie reminded me that I had to pick up Jonathan's belongings from his apartment in Brooklyn, New York. She was adamant that I not drive myself. Robin and Angel also discouraged me from handling this task alone and offered to accompany me. I agreed. It was the right decision since I cried the entire ride.

Jonathan's personal items were already packed and sitting on the bed where he slept. I sat on the bed and cried, wanting to stay in the room. Jonathan's landlord handed me an envelope containing his security deposit and extra money Jonathan asked her to hold for him. I was so proud of my son and surprised. I thanked his landlord; I was grateful for her acts of kindness and honesty. She would always have a place in my heart.

After leaving Jonathan's apartment, we stopped at 110th Street and Central Park, where we had stopped 34 years ago as freshmen in college riding to Syracuse. A couple graciously relinquished a park bench so that we could take a picture. We sat on the bench, took a selfie, and reminisced when life was easy. For a moment, I was smiling and forgot about the reason for the trip.

We had lunch in Manhattan, laughing about Angel getting mad after the Broadway show and the hotel we stayed at in Times Square. Hours later, we returned to New Haven, and they drove back to Boston. At that moment, I was feeling thankful for them being in my life and for our true friendship.

Nightfall came and I was back on my knees crying to God. I received a text from Nurse Betty telling me to please get some rest. I quickly learned that Betty was a quiet, albeit caring Facebook stalker, reading my posts and thereby keeping track of my whereabouts and how I was handling everything. One weekend Nurse Betty arranged and provided another Reiki session in her office. After the session, she reported that I was stubborn, and she still had difficulties moving the blood flow from my head. At home, once again I fell asleep on my knees, crying and asking God the same questions.

ANSWERED PRAYERS

While I was asleep, God finally answered one of my questions. In my dream, God sent an angel appearing as Pastor Bennett, someone I trusted, respected, and to whom I would listen. Pastor Bennett was dressed in his signature all-white, Afro-centric clothing. The godly image of Pastor Bennett appeared on the lighted side in my dream, standing on the water, but neither his feet nor pants legs were wet. In the dream, I was standing on solid ground on the darker side across from him. Pastor Bennett said, "What do you want?" His tone of voice seemed annoyed, as a parent would respond to a child who kept calling his name.

In the dream, I looked at the godly image and said, "Where is my son?"

"He's with me. What else do you want?" replied the spiritual figure who looked like my pastor.

It was like He was saying, Minister Cooper, seminary graduate, why are you asking me questions to which you already know the answers?

"I don't know," I replied.

He responded, "When you find out, ask." Pointing down to my right side, He continued, "But, you should be concentrating on her."

When I looked down, there was my daughter, prostrate on the ground. There was a darkness over her in the dream. She never raised her head or moved. I woke up in the middle of the night relieved my son was with God, but I forgot to ask Him why He didn't save my son. I wondered how God could answer my questions and make me feel stupid for asking them. At least I had a partial answer.

I immediately walked downstairs to check on my daughter. The moment I hit the bottom of the stairs the smell of weed hit me like a ton of bricks. I stood there fussing with myself and silently at my daughter. What the heck is this smell? This chick knows I don't allow smoking in my house, especially weed. Furious at the thought, the audacity of my daughter, I kept walking. Grief or no grief, there is no smoking in my house. Every step closer to her door, the smell was more pungent, and my anger rose. As I reached her bathroom door, I noticed empty brandy bottles in the bathroom trash can. I pushed her door open. Empty cups were on her dresser, and her room smelled like an ashtray, just nasty. It dawned on me I had not really seen or heard much from my daughter since Jonathan's death.

I stood in the doorway, numb, confused and angry. I wanted to kick Jackie's bed and pull her out of it onto the floor. I could hear the bell ringing, indicating it was time to fight. Before I opened my mouth, a calmness flushed through my body. Flashes of me sitting at the bar drinking and rumbling through my cabinet for pills all came flashing through my mind. Jackie moved and peeked from beneath the layers of blankets. She hurried to hide the bottle on the nightstand.

Walking calmly and scared again, I sat down on her bed, looking at her but barely recognizing my princess. Jackie had fallen asleep in her clothes. Her eyes were sad and puffy, with dark rings around them. Her skin and lips were cracked and dry, her locks all over her head and in need of care. This woman was not the radiant and beautiful daughter I called Princess. Sitting next to her, I could smell the alcohol, which seemed to ooze from her pores. There was a joint in her ashtray. My daughter saw me staring at it and tried to cover it up. Despite my rules about smoking and weed being off-limits in the house, this time, I didn't say anything about what I saw.

Instead, sitting on her bed, at that moment, believing myself to be a failure to both my children, I told Jackie about my dream. She listened. Retelling my dream to Jackie felt very spiritual and surreal. I thought about how often God sent angels as messengers through dreams. An angel spoke to Joseph about the immaculate conception. An angel told Zechariah his wife, Elizabeth, was pregnant. Joseph interpreted dreams to save Israel during the seven-year drought. And now, 3,000 years later, God spoke to me, a Black woman living in an urban-suburban community in New Haven, to alert me about my Black child, my daughter. When I finished talking, Jackie sat up straighter in the bed and cleared her throat.

"I've been watching you come home every night and disappear upstairs until morning," she said, slowly and in a low tone. "You stopped talking to me and haven't noticed your granddaughter or me. I have been watching you withdraw from everyone, and it's been painful. You lost a son, I lost a brother, and losing you has been too much for me to carry."

For the first time since Jonathan died, I listened. My daughter told me that since the article appeared in the New Haven Register with the photograph of her, Jonathan and me at the culinary school, people who recognized her began approaching her with words of sympathy and condolence.

"I tried to focus on work, then someone would come in and say, 'Aren't you the girl on the cover of the newspaper?' They either knew Jonathan or would tell me how messed up it was that he was murdered. It was too much!" she said.

Listening to her relay the pain and anguish she was experiencing was heart-wrenching for me as her mother. My purpose in having the New Haven Register write the article was to help remove the negative stigma people had about the death of Black men. The most difficult words to hear were those from my daughter telling me that I had not considered her feelings and she could not let the pain go. She blamed me every day, and every time someone stared in her direction, the anger returned. Jackie told me that the only thing keeping her sane was her daughter.

"She's all I have. If it weren't for Maya, I would have left the state, and you would have lost me too," Jackie told me through tears.

Jackie, who was alive and living in the same house with me, was in pain, and I had been oblivious to her needs. As Jackie was talking, I realized that God answered one of my questions four years ago. I asked Him, "Why was Jackie pregnant and having a child out of wedlock?" God was telling me that my granddaughter was born to save my daughter's life. God answers questions in His time. Hopefully, God will share why my son died.

Jackie and I talked for a while that morning. She agreed to finish culinary school—graduation was approaching in less than six months—in January 2017. We also agreed that after graduation, she would take time off from work, allowing her space and time to mourn her brother.

How could I have ignored my child? We worked together, lived in the same house, and she was invisible to me. My pain and anger from losing Jonathan had consumed my entire existence. For the first time in months, I thanked God for the dream and the ability to save my daughter and begin to restore our shattered relationship.

The following morning, I phoned Rev. Anderson to discuss my dream and my conversation with Jackie. Rev. Anderson listened and was thankful that God was answering prayers. At the end of the conversation, she suggested that I do something to honor my son's memory and his life. Confused by the suggestion, I did not ask how or why.

CHAPTER 11
INTERRUPTION: SOCIAL JUSTICE: SHUT IT DOWN!

IT WAS GREAT TO WAKE UP to a Saturday morning with no work, and I could sleep. Turning on the television in my room, I heard the newscaster announce that a Black man was shot outside Poppy's Pizza Bar in Hamden at 1:30 a.m. Such announcements were becoming standard for the New Haven local news station on Saturday mornings. This time, I was not immune to the news. Bending over in pain, gripping my stomach, I fell straight to my knees. I cried tears as if they were talking about my son again. All I could think was, "This has to stop! How can we prevent this from happening? This is becoming entirely too painful. I wondered how I could help another mother not wake up the way I did.

After sitting on the floor for a moment, holding my stomach and rocking back and forth, I looked over at my phone and decided it was time to do something different. I called Matt, the lead organizer for CONECT (Congregations Organized for a New Connecticut), a collective of churches, synagogues, mosques, temples, and civic organizations from New Haven and Fairfield counties that joined together to address social and economic justice issues. The group represented more than 20,000 people from different races and faith backgrounds who lived in both cities and suburbs. I had been a member of the organization in various iterations for more than 20 years.

I updated Matt on the latest shooting and asked him how we could stop the violence at Poppy's and prevent another mother from experiencing this pain. Matt was empathetic to the call but unsure how to respond. He agreed to vet my call to action to the executive and strategy team. I hung up from Matt, hopeful and prayerful that we could find a way to stop the violence.

Two weeks later, Matt called to report that CONECT members were supportive of this new effort to stop the violence and there were already helpful suggestions. After some investigation, one member discovered we could challenge the bar's liquor license, which was up for renewal soon. However, Matt cautioned that we would have to work fast.

"A lawyer has volunteered to represent us in court," he said. "But this is going to take at least eight months to resolve. We must schedule meetings with the mayor, police chief, and the president of Southern Connecticut State University and review all the police reports about shootings and complaints against Poppy's. Then we must convince other allies to support us.

"Phil has already done a power analysis on successful cases where an establishment was closed, and those cases had the police chief and mayor's support," he continued. "We have to schedule a press conference, meet with the owner of Poppy's, and then file a claim with the Liquor License Commissioner before the owner renews the liquor license. Once a hearing is scheduled, the owners are notified, and then we can challenge their renewal in court."

Matt told me the mayor and police chief already promised their support. He then expressed the group's concern that I was taking on too much too soon.

"It's only been five months since your son was murdered. Are you sure you are ready for this? It will not bring your son back, but we are willing to take on this action," he said.

A meeting was subsequently scheduled with Hamden's mayor and eight members from CONECT. The mayor walked in carrying a manila folder and eyeing us as if we were a bunch of community religious leaders ready to chastise him for not doing enough to de-escalate crime in the city. He sat down and immediately began talking about programs his administrative team was prepared to implement and the success of some of the programs already in place. Matt politely interrupted the mayor to suggest we all introduce ourselves, which we did. I was the last person to do so. I was teary-eyed but made a concerted effort to compose myself and control my voice to sound strong and assertive.

I told the mayor that I was the mother of Jonathan Cooper, who was gunned down outside of Poppy's Pizza Bar on April 23.

"It seems as if every Friday night we hear about the shooting of another Black man outside that bar," I said. "We are here to help you stop the violence. We want to know how we can help you shut this place down!"

The mayor's demeanor and facial expression changed. His voice was more compassionate in extending his condolences to me and acknowledging the last family photo taken with Jonathan. He then cautioned us to act fast if we wanted to challenge the bar's liquor license renewal in court. We needed 10 signatures from Hamden residents and witnesses willing to testify in court about the level of crime and violence they personally witnessed outside Poppy's on Friday nights. He advised us we would need the cooperation of the Hamden Police Department and its chief.

The mayor confirmed that in response to previous 911 calls related to Poppy's, the city had solicited the support of Southern Connecticut State University security officials to help deal with the crime in the area on Friday nights. Before the meeting ended, the mayor called the police chief to schedule a meeting between him and our group. We left the mayor's office feeling optimistic about the next steps.

Two days later, we met with the Hamden police chief. He provided us with helpful information about crime in the area. We received stacks of 911 calls reporting shootings, underage drinking, drugs sold and stored in pizza boxes, destruction of property, and theft and vandalism of cars. We learned that freshmen at Southern Connecticut State University were cautioned to avoid the area around the pizza bar, especially on Friday nights. The chief promised the complete support of his department in our efforts.

The following week CONECT scheduled a press conference outside of Poppy's with the mayor and police chief present. Standing

with us were my sorority sisters, a few current and previous coworkers, one family member, and religious and community supporters.
Standing on the outskirts were a handful of reporters. Specifically,
CONECT announced it was moving forward with legal efforts to
prevent Poppy's liquor license renewal.

The next night, five CONECT members met at the Dunkin' Donuts in Hamden to discuss how we would begin canvassing the community for signatures. We agreed to split into teams and knock on
the doors of residents living within a seven-block radius of Poppy's
Pizza Bar. Initially, we believed that canvassing the neighborhood for
signatures would be an easy journey. Instead, as we knocked on door
after door, we heard story after story of families whose cars were van-
dalized, bottles thrown at homes, and bullets flying through front
windows. The noise, disruption, and disrespect caused by patrons of
the pizza bar on Friday nights had traumatized this entire community.

We heard many troubling stories. A couple was enjoying a peace-
ful Friday night watching television until a bullet came through the
window. They dove to the floor to avoid being hit. The bullet landed
in the wall. The father went into their children's bedrooms, pulling
them to the floor, while the mother carefully moved to the back of
the house and called 911. They were petrified until the police arrived.
I could see the fear and pain in this mother's eyes. She told me she
and her husband rearranged the children's room, lowering the bunk
beds. On Friday nights, they now live in the back of their house and
are constantly afraid.

We heard from a mother who did not allow her teenagers to come
home on Friday nights, fearing somebody would shoot them. She
insisted her kids spend the night at friends' homes. There were many
more of these stories of trauma, all heart-wrenching.

We ended the night back at Dunkin' Donuts, where we shared the
stories we heard. I was mentally exhausted and heartbroken that the
police allowed this type of activity to occur in a neighborhood for all
these years, seemingly unable to stop the violence. The people of this
community were living under siege in their homes. Oddly, I had a
sense of hope we would be able to make a difference.

With all of the needed signatures, our lawyer scheduled a hearing date in a Hartford court. On the first day of the hearing, the courtroom and hallways were packed. In attendance were officials, clergy, community residents, and members of the Saint Rose of Lima Church in New Haven, some of whom were undocumented workers. When I walked into the lobby, several people met me with smiles and words of support: "We are here because we love you, Odell."

One member from St. Lima's church told me, "I remembered when you stood with us to challenge the state on allowing our undocumented children to attend local colleges, pay in-state tuition, and receive driver's licenses. I know this won't bring your son back, but we are here for you." We hugged, and I thanked all of them from my heart.

Shortly before the hearing began, Matt approached me to relay some concerning news. The police chief was demanding that I not testify or share my story about Jonathan. The case was an open, unsolved murder case, and they could not risk me divulging any confidential information. I was angry and felt cheated that I was forced to be voiceless, but I did not have a choice. The hearings lasted over two months. The lawyer called Hamden residents, the mayor and the police chief to testify. It was grueling and painful listening to the lawyer for Poppy's blame the violence on the community.

One month after the hearings concluded, I received the exciting news that the commission did not renew Poppy's liquor license. I excitedly thanked Matt and Phil for their commitment. I knew this would not solve all gun violence issues, but at least another mother would not receive a call that her son got shot outside of Poppy's. Three months later, Poppy's officially closed, and the neighborhood could live a new life of freedom.

Of course, as with any issue, there are two sides, and everyone was not pleased about the closing. Other than Friday nights, Poppy's was a decent place to eat and watch Sunday football. In addition, the closure resulted in Poppy's employees losing their jobs, and Matt was correct, the bar closing didn't bring my son back or lessen the pain.

At a church service in Hamden after Poppy's closed, a mother gave her testimony, praising God for answering her prayers. Poppy's was closed, and her family was safer. I felt a sense of warmth and humility that God chose me as the catalyst to rouse a community to demand a change. Initially embarking on this issue because of my son's murder, his name or my voice were never heard. The community trusted us and liberated itself.

CHAPTER 12

INTERRUPTION: NEW NORMAL

RETURNING TO MY NEW NORMAL AND reviewing my to-do list, I realized I need-ed to finally cancel my son's cellphone. Occasionally, I found myself calling the number just to hear his voice. Then I would cry and hang up. The detective had given me permission weeks before to cancel the account. When I called AT&T to close the account, the representa-tive asked if I was calling to report it lost again. I had a flashback to Jonathan in high school.

After the YouTube/ex-girlfriend/stuffed animal/red bandanas epi-sode, part of Jonathan's punishment was he could not use technology. He placed his laptop and cellphone on the table.

"Technically, mom, I paid for this cellphone and should be able to keep it," he said.

I couldn't believe my ears! Jonathan was trying to punk me after all this. Powerless at the moment, I took his laptop upstairs and placed it in my room. However, I was not going to get punked by my child. So, I waited until I knew he was using his phone and sending text messages. I phoned AT&T, reported the cellphone missing, and asked them to disconnect the service until it was located.

"Mom, something is wrong with my phone," he complained the following morning when he came out of his room. "I was texting last night, and it just cut off."

I looked at him and smiled. "You may have paid for the phone, but I pay for the service," I said.

John dropped his head and said, "You got me."

Jackie, laughing in her room, told Jonathan, "You still haven't learned. She will never let you win."

My theory was that God looked after single mothers. But this phone call was different. I told the AT&T representative that my son was murdered, and the police had his phone as evidence. She apologized, closed the account, and erased all back charges beginning April 23. I then canceled all his credit cards and called the school and student loan company to inform them of Jonathan Cooper's death. Once they all received the death certificate, the accounts would be closed, and no further payment expected. Paying on a student loan would have been horrifying and torture. However, although the student loan company forgave the debt, it appeared as income earned, and consequently, I owed taxes on over $20,000. I was grateful for having a great tax accountant that year. The only account I left in Jonathan's name was Netflix. For some reason, I didn't mind receiving emails that said, "Jonathan, look what's new coming to Netflix." My son introduced me to Netflix and streaming. Taking his name off the account seemed selfish.

TOO SOON TO CELEBRATE LIFE

In November, Jonathan would have been 25 years old. Jackie convinced me that we needed to have a party to celebrate and honor her brother's life. I was against it, but I wanted to support her journey of healing. However, what we intended as a joyful celebration of Jonathan's life, turned into a disaster. I learned that night that alcohol does not mask the pain, hurt, and anger felt when you lose somebody so close so fast.

It dawned on me that I hadn't seen or spoken much to Marcel and Damar in the seven months since Jonathan's death. I guess they were wrestling with the murder of their brother and were not coping well. I was sad I couldn't help them or be more supportive. It seemed as if all of us were falling into the same endless rabbit hole. If I was going to save my family, I had to save myself first. Now I understood the flight attendants' instruction to airline passengers to place the oxygen mask on yourself first before trying to save others.

STIGMAS AND MYTHS

In my family, we were taught to keep our problems to ourselves, remain private and don't tell strangers our business. We were advised to pray more and that Black people did not seek counseling. Our ancestors survived slavery without counseling, and you can, too. When I was married, we attempted marriage counseling a few times. Those sessions only put a bandage on the wound when we apparently needed surgery. If this counseling was going to work, I would need to be honest and truthful about everything I had experienced and was confused about since my son's murder. It was time to disrupt my silence and break through the years of the myths and stigmas of seeking a counselor.

Monday morning, I phoned a trauma counselor, Dr. Hadar, for an appointment. The first visits were uncomfortable, but I promised myself to be honest. And because we met in a leadership group, Dr. Hadar was prepared and knew she had to be straightforward, respect my faith, and be brutally honest. She was excellent at her job and could call me out on my bullshit. "Odell, I disagree with your thinking and I need you to change your language and perspective," she advised me on one occasion. "You lost your son traumatically and what you are experiencing is not normal. Your symptoms and behavior are being driven by something biological happening in your body. You may think you have control, but you don't. And I am glad you came to counseling."

By the fourth session, she asked that I respond to a series of questions to validate her suspicion I had PTSD and depression. The questions were: Did I have periods of sadness and anxiety? Did I have feelings of hopelessness, helplessness, worthlessness, and guilt? Did I have a loss of interest in activities I once found pleasurable? Had I experienced fatigue or insomnia, a noticeable decrease in energy, feelings of anxiety and difficulty concentrating? Did I have a reduction in appetite? And finally, did I have momentary thoughts of suicide? After answering "yes" to all the questions posed, she diagnosed me with PTSD and depression. She recommended I take medication.

Again, another red flag. I could hear my family saying, "Don't take the medication. Stay off pills. Black people don't need pills. The first thing a doctor wants to give you is a pill." I shook those comments out of my head, took a deep breath and before agreeing to take the recommended medicine, as a first step, I had to complete my research on the depression medication she recommended. We agreed to allow me a week before saying "yes."

When I returned to work, a culinary student suddenly died from an asthma attack. He was in class on Friday and died Saturday. His death was a wake-up call. Tomorrow was not promised to anyone. When I returned to the trauma counselor, I agreed to take the prescribed medication. A week later, one of my sorority sisters invited me to dinner. For the first time in months, I could get out of bed without feeling sluggish and feeling doom and gloom. I guess the medication was working.

In January, Jackie graduated from culinary school and, as we agreed, she took time off to finally grieve her brother's death. While she was home, she noticed a profound change in my behavior. I was repetitive in my communication, and my memory was worse. She waited for the right time to tell me she didn't recognize her mother. Her observation was contrary to how I felt. Finally, I was able to wake up in the morning without feeling sluggish or anxious. I was returning phone calls and reconnecting with people. However, she claimed she did not recognize me and our communication was awkward. Jackie did not want me to depend on pills to function. I don't know what part of my behavior was scary, but she saw something in me that was not her mother. She begged me to stop taking the medication and learn to make decisions and reclaim my life another way. During our discussion, I promised to wean myself off the pill before reaching the six-month mark. Based on the research, after six months, I would not be able to stop taking the medication.

By the end of March, I was no longer employed at ConnCAT. Reflecting on the last months of Coop's murder, I should not have returned to work.

Some years ago, I read a book by Dr. Joy DeGruy, called Post Traumatic Slave Syndrome. In the book Dr. DeGruy readily defined symptoms consistent with PTSD and Post Traumatic Stress Syndrome (PTSS) that are now acknowledged as serious health issues. Even so, PTSS often goes unrecognized until an official diagnosis of PTSD is made. PTSD results from a single trauma experienced directly or indirectly. PTSS, on the other hand, is from people experiencing racism through the generations as well as individuals facing constant stress from everyday racism.

In summary, the adaptative behaviors our ancestors developed from slavery had been passed down through generations. The behaviors that were passed down from my family were to keep your pain to yourself, return to work, and try harder, regardless of the traumatic interruption in your life. I believed all the hype of being a strong Black woman and I would get through this. Well, if you learn nothing else from my story, please remember this. What was going on in my body was biological (PTSD, depression, PTSS and more). Although I looked like myself on the outside and when people asked me what was wrong, I was taught to reply, "Nothing, I am fine," I was not fine. I was far from feeling fine. It was the 20th century and I still responded with an enslaved mentality of just return to work and keep busy. This was the wrong thing to do! I began blaming others for my mistakes and blaming everyone for my confusion. I could not see myself. My presence at home and work was toxic and colorfully explosive.

Someone should have made me take a personal leave of absence from work and make all my financial and life decisions until I was mentally capable of managing my mental health. If this is you, my advice is to get help, break the silence and find someone to lean on. The problem is biological, compounded by years of hearing our ancestors' teachings on how people of color should respond to trauma. Because they didn't receive counseling doesn't mean we shouldn't.

After leaving the job, I went home, paid my bills for the month, learned how to file for unemployment, and balanced my bank account. When Jackie returned from work, I gave her the news and told her that I was going to bed. I was mentally and physically exhausted. However, I told her that I would need a job by June 1.

I staggered up the stairs to my bedroom. Tossing my work clothes in the corner, I put on Jonathan's black sweatpants and Wavy Gang T-shirt and crashed on my bed. I did not want light, television, or music. I laid in the middle of my bed, which seemed to be pulling me down. Every emotion, every tear, every pain was just seeping through the mattress. It was holding me, and I could not move. I don't know how long I was there. I don't remember eating or drinking, just going to the bathroom and back to my bed. I heard Jackie coming up the stairs, asking me if I wanted something to eat or drink. But I had no consciousness of time or day. I wasn't hungry. Jackie would bring me a cup of tea in the morning, and when it got pitch dark in my room at night, I noticed it was gone. Occasionally I would wake up, look around the room and realize that I didn't have to go to work, and I would just cry. I cried some more.

On April 1, 2017, Jackie and I both began our emotional meltdown. The entire month was our trigger. I refused to acknowledge the day of Jonathan's death, only his day of birth. However, April 23 is always a heart-wrenching day. I could not explain the anxiety or mood swings. They just happened. I planned to be alone and cry; depression had control of my emotions. I could succumb to it or find an alternative way to live. Unfortunately, depression won, and I was going to stay home alone. However, Angel and Robin drove down from Boston for the weekend to make sure I wasn't alone. The moment they arrived we left the house. We dined at three different restaurants. One was the last place Jonathan and I had dinner together. This time, I sat at a booth and stared at the table. We treated ourselves to a manicure and pedicure in neighboring Orange, Connecticut, and headed downtown for desserts. The chef sent out a tray of special desserts, and we ate all of them. While there, a former coworker and his husband stopped and had a drink with us.

We talked and laughed all weekend as they tried their best to keep me preoccupied and feeling thankful for the life I had. Angel and Robin left Sunday afternoon, and I was grateful for the visit. Sitting in my living room, I said, "Look at God, Satan lost again."

I didn't see Jackie much that weekend; she decided to work. Damar and Marcel were absent. They did not enjoy coming to the house anymore, and we only spoke by text message. The messages were always short with the added smiling emoji face and a promise to visit. I hadn't personally spent time with them and was missing their company. They never wanted to talk about their feelings or the loss of their brother. Jackie was still drinking and trying to hide the bottles in the house. I drank as well, but socially. I would stop by the bar near my home for happy hour and enjoy a Carmel Appletini and Buffalo Chicken Quesadilla, both of which were always comforting.

Days later, I had a follow-up meeting with Dr. Hadar, during which we discussed a plan to wean me off the depression medication. I shared the details of how I spent the weekend with my friends from Boston. I was honest in reporting the dark dreams had returned and my anxiety had tripled. I was attending church regularly and praying for deliverance. She suggested I stop attending happy hour. Drinking alcoholic beverages with the depression medication was not a smart combination, regardless of how much I prayed. She was glad to hear that Jackie would be nearby during my transition off the pill. However, I was beginning to feel like I was a burden to Jackie.

I was in constant prayer for strength during the transition. Occasionally, just when I needed a boost, soror IGotcha would send a spiritual quote to help me through the day. Jackie wanted me to be completely free of the pill; I didn't want to disappoint her again. I couldn't keep her brother safe, but I could stop taking the depression medication if my behavior was so scary.

Friends encouraged me to remain on the medication, believing it helped manage a balanced life. I learned not to judge anyone who needed the pill to obtain a better quality of life. However, my personal goal was to honor Jackie's wish and regain some sense of normalcy.

The following month was challenging, but the dark dreams subsided. I thanked Jesus for being present and carrying me through the darkness so I wouldn't get lost. Psalm 23:4 had new meaning.

"Though I walk through the valley of the shadow of death, I will fear no evil: for thou art with me; thy rod and thy staff they comfort me."

No matter how angry I was with God, Jesus was always there to save me. Six weeks later, I was completely weaned off the pill.

One morning I woke up with Jackie and Marcel standing in my bedroom, calling my name, checking on me to see if I was OK. Jackie informed me that I had been in my room alone, and I again told her that I needed a job by June or we were going to be broke. She informed me that it was May. I had no concept of time or day. I didn't realize how tired I was, how exhausted I was. I know I ate. I know I drank. But I just don't remember doing anything. Time seemed to get away from me. Jackie encouraged me to get up and return phone calls. My sorority sisters had been calling her and hitting her up on Facebook, concerned about me since I was not returning any phone calls. When I looked at the phone, I had many unread emails, text messages and missed calls. I saw a message from my sorority sister IGotcha about a job posting that was "perfect for you."

Later that night, I opened up the job post and realized it was a perfect job. The job was in Connecticut, and an application was due immediately. Checkbox helped me to update my resume and write a cover letter.

I landed an interview and was later offered the position starting June 1, 2017. During the onboarding orientation, the human resources director wanted to confirm that I was without health insurance. When I validated her question, she informed me that the CEO gave her permission to fast-track my benefits and provided me with healthcare effective immediately. Company benefits included life insurance, short-term disability, and paid vacation, which would be available after 90 days of employment. Fighting back the tears of joy, I greeted the CEO when he walked in to meet me. Before I left the parking lot, I phoned both my sorority sisters and shared the good news. I was employed—with benefits! On the 45-minute ride back to New Haven, I thanked Jesus for His grace and mercy. I felt that Jesus was advocating on my behalf to God. It was becoming a little more difficult to remain mad at God, but I still wanted to know why He didn't save my son. Looking at the bright side, I had secured employment and was heading home with good news.

CHAPTER 13
INTERRUPTION: NEW JOB ... MORE STRESS

I WAS THANKFUL TO HAVE NEW employment. Although the main office was a 45-minute drive from my home, my office was 20 minutes away, making the drive to work relatively smooth. Although I was familiar with this office and most of the staff, I was unfamiliar with the work culture. Unfortunately, it did not take long to detect that it was toxic. The environment was tense. When the director introduced me as the new manager, the reaction was welcoming. However, although I could not place my finger on it at the time, I seemed to notice raised eyebrows and facial expressions that may not have been so welcoming. I knew something might warrant my attention.

For the next couple of weeks, I closely observed people's behavior and listened to their conversations. Occasionally, someone would walk by my office and comment that they were surprised to see my office door always open. The surprise was because my predecessor kept the door closed, so this was a pleasant and welcomed change.

In my first two months in this new position, the office went through a significant downsizing and reorganization of the hourly staff. On more than one occasion, employees confidentially advised me to be careful during this process because certain employees had special privileges and favor with management. A few weeks into the reorganization, it became clear which employees had the full favor of the management team and others who had none. The distinctions did not particularly seem fair.

At times I sat in my office and wondered why I was hired.

However, with the spirit of Harriet Tubman boiling in my spirit I was able to intervene in one situation successfully. A beautiful Black, middle-aged woman, whom I will call Grace to preserve her privacy, came into my office, politely introduced herself, and sat down. I shut the door. Looking into her eyes, I could tell she was tired and carrying stress. She was doing her best to present herself as a strong Black woman. I asked if we could have a confidential conversation about her recent attendance issues. Holding back the tears, she opened up and shared her medical challenges, specifically securing doctor appointments before work hours and receiving treatments after hours. Listening to her discuss having to choose between health and work was troublesome.

Grace permitted me to speak with her primary doctor, and we arranged a schedule for appointments and medical treatments. All I had to do was gain approval to shift her start time back 30 minutes every day. I knew the director would disapprove, so I phoned our HR department. The HR director was aware of the medical history but not the challenges of her securing the necessary appointments. I received approval to shift her work hours but I went a step further and asked if we could protect Grace from being downsized because of attendance warnings. Grace needed the full-time hours to qualify for healthcare, not only for her but also for her husband, who also had medical issues. The HR director agreed and thanked me for calling. She agreed to protect Grace from being downsized. Grace left my office with a huge burden removed from her shoulders and hopeful about receiving the medical treatment needed to restore her quality of life.

The director subsequently chastised me for my efforts; however, I knew I had done the right thing. Despite this victory, the office environment remained toxic—until the director was removed and temporarily replaced with another director from a different region. We experienced two months of mutual respect, support and fair treatment. However, we were then informed that on November 30, 2017, everyone (hourly employees and management staff) would be unemployed. Without a job meant without healthcare. My time on this job had been extremely stressful. Now the news of my impending unemployment coupled with the police investigation of Jonathan's murder was too much.

CHAPTER 14
INTERRUPTION: THIS IS TOO MUCH

JACKIE AND I WERE BOTH LEARNING how to adjust to our new ways of life. We argued and disagreed more, and I was not going to be yelled at in my house. In the past, Jonathan was the bridge mending our conflicts. Depending on the severity of the disagreement, he would come home from New York and just be present for Jackie and me. Eventually, the issue causing the argument was unimportant, and all was well. However, this was different with Jonathan gone. We both became angry over the smallest things in the house. Who was going to clean the only glass in the sink, or who used the last clean fork in the house? We both missed Jonathan, didn't talk about it to each other and could not find a compromise on how to live together.

One day during breakfast, my granddaughter stood up in a dining room chair and pointed her finger at Jackie and me arguing in the kitchen.

"Please stop arguing. It makes me uncomfortable," she said. "You two need to find a better way to communicate."

Jackie and I were startled by the scolding from a child and laughed. We knew the comment came from her Uncle Jonathan and we promised to improve our behavior and communication.

That Sunday, the Jehovah's Witness returned. I could not understand why this woman faithfully returned twice a month to be a victim of my pain. This visit was slightly better. My anger was not as harsh, but the pain was still present. When she asked if I had returned to teaching at Hartford Seminary, I explained I was not in the spirit to teach about healing, miracles and Jesus saving peoples' lives. A strange look crossed her face. However, I believe she was trying to understand my healing journey.

The detectives investigating Coop's murder phoned and wanted to come by the house and introduce the new Bureau of Alcohol, Tobacco and Firearms detectives. It appeared it was now a federal case because the suspects were involved in interstate crimes. There were new developments, and they needed additional information from Jackie and me. Also, the detective told us they could not contact my nephew Skeeter and wanted our help. Emphasizing the importance of speaking with Skeeter as soon as possible, he asked if I could call my sister and help expedite their conversation with her son.

I phoned Charlene, who was in Boston at a funeral. When she answered, through the pain and tears I began pouring my heart out. I told my sister everything the detective told me about the case and how important the next few days were for the evidentiary presentation to the grand jury to have the best chance for a conviction of the young men who murdered my son, her nephew. I couldn't remember a time in my life when I needed my big sister more. I do not think I had ever begged my sister for anything. I never needed her for anything other than not to tell Momma Doe that I broke something or quietly stayed on the phone past my 10 p.m. curfew.

"Sis, that's it. That is why the detectives need to talk to Skeeter," I said, taking a deep breath.

Charlene told me Skeeter was out of town and did not have an internet connection, or she would phone him. Then she conveyed the most comforting, positive sentiment I had ever heard in my life.

"I got you. I'll take care of it as soon as I get home," she said. "I promise that I'm here for you. We'll get through this together."

Tears rolled down my cheeks, and I hung up, feeling a big sigh of relief. My job was ending, and the murder investigation was extremely stressful, so this conversation with Charlene was helpful.

The following day, my phone rang, and it was Charlene. I smiled at the thought she was calling me back this quickly. When I answered the phone, she asked whether Jonathan's case had been solved. I was confused and disturbed by the question, considering our previous conversation. She wondered why ATF detectives rather than the local detectives had left their cards at her house. I explained the situation again, and she promised to have Skeeter call when he got home.

When the detective called early in the morning two days later, I was sure they finally spoke with Skeeter and had what they needed for the grand jury. I picked up the phone with a sense of energy and relief. My relief was short-lived as the detective wanted to meet in person. They had not talked to Skeeter.

Before the end of the day, the detective called again and left a message saying we no longer needed to meet. Skeeter posted on Facebook that he was out of the state and was not talking to any police. My heart skipped a few beats, but before I could finish viewing the message, the detective called back. I was annoyed.

"What?" I asked sharply into the phone.

The detective informed me the ATF detectives intended to call Skeeter's cellphone and demand he return to Connecticut. He also said the delay in speaking to Skeeter was creating problems for their case before the grand jury. Again, I asked if Skeeter's life would be at risk by answering his questions and the detective said, "Absolutely not." It didn't matter how much I wanted this case solved; it could not be at the risk of his life.

The detective also mentioned the police chief had prohibited him from sharing additional information with me about this case. They were concerned about gathering all the information they needed before the grand jury convened.

Before hanging up, he said he had the authority to tell me another person who would cooperate and answer their questions had been identified. The person was coming into the federal building the following morning. The detective could not tell me who this person was but stressed their commitment to finding justice in Jonathan's murder. My stress level hit a new high. The thought of being unemployed again was unimaginable. I carried this stress alone and was looking forward to meeting with Dr. Hadar to discuss it. I wanted a drink!

On the morning of November 14, 2017, I was preparing for work.

The sun was shining, and I wore a bright green dress to raise my spirits. Just as I was stepping into my car, I was hit with the worst headache in my life. I staggered backward and fell to the grass. My vision was blurry, my stomach was queasy, and I was about to vomit. Running back into the house just in time, I sat on the bathroom floor. The headache and stiff neck did not subside. I texted Jackie to come home; she had just taken Maya to school. Moments later, she arrived worried because she found my purse was in my car and the driver's door open. Giving her my cellphone, I told her to call my job. There wasn't any way I could drive. I asked her for a pill for a migraine headache or Sudafed. Unable to move my head or body, I fell asleep on the couch. I awoke around 4:30 in the afternoon when she was leaving to pick up my granddaughter from school. Concerned, Jackie suggested I call the doctor or go to the emergency room. Instead, I went upstairs to bed, promising her if the headache and nausea didn't subside in the morning, I would see Dr. Edward. When I awakened again, it was 4 a.m., and the pain was worse. It was too early to call Dr. Edward for an appointment. I laid back down until the alarm rang at 8 a.m. It took me an hour to get dressed. I could barely speak, but I called Dr. Edward's office for an emergency appointment.

Today was Jonathan's birthday, and as I left for the doctor's office, I found three helium happy birthday balloons, four candles, and a bouquet of flowers on the porch. The unknown "phantom" was at it again. The phantom never left a card or note—the same thing happened last year—just the same arrangement. They made me cry. I was touched by this continuing commitment to honor Jonathan.

Driving myself to the doctor's office was excruciating. When Dr. Edward arrived a few minutes later, he was curious about why the lights were out. He immediately began asking what happened. I could see his facial expression change from relaxed to worried. He held my right hand and had me push on his hand, then he grabbed my left hand and said push. The tears began running down my face. My left hand was numb, and his touch felt like fire streaming into my arm.

"I need to send you to the emergency room now. You need a series of tests, and the fastest way to have them completed is in the ER," Dr. Edward said and stepped back.

Trying to avoid the cost of an ambulance fee, I suggested I could drive. Dr. Edward did not argue; he just responded with an emphatic, "NO!"

The next thing I remembered was leaving his office on a stretcher. For the first time in 20 years, I left his office without making jokes. Dr. Edward gave the paramedics strict instructions on what to relay to the medical staff when I arrived at the hospital.

Yale-New Haven Hospital had now acquired both local hospitals. I suggested they take me to the St. Raphael's Campus instead of the main hospital because I knew too many people there. Meanwhile, riding in the back of the ambulance, I sent several texts, including one to my daughter, telling her what I knew to that point, and one to Brenda, asking her to meet me at the ER.

Once I arrived at the ER, the paramedics gave the ER nurse some information about my health. Not considering my case a priority, she instructed me to sit in the waiting room. The light was painful, and the pain had not subsided. Brenda showed up, and we sat in the waiting room for another 30 minutes before I was rolled into an exam room. After answering all the medical insurance questions, I was transported down the hall for a CAT scan. The nurse said it sounded like I had meningitis, and they needed to isolate me from others. I didn't know what meningitis was, but I thought a shot would clear it up. After lying in an exam room by myself, the doctor returned. I did not have meningitis, she said. I was bleeding in my brain. She called it an aneurysm. They were transporting me to the main hospital. The ride was 10 minutes. I sent a final text telling everyone that I was about to have brain surgery.

"I am bleeding in my head," I wrote and pressed the send button.

As I arrived at the Yale ER, Jackie called my cellphone. Four people in white coats were waiting outside the door for my arrival. I immediately knew something was wrong. It was like a scene from Grey's Anatomy when the doctors were pre-warned about a critical case. Jackie asked if she should come down. Before I could respond, I asked the doctor about how long I would be in the hospital.

"My daughter wants to know if she should come down."

Looking very confused, he held my hand and replied, "A minimum of three weeks."

Trying to hold back my fear, I told Jackie, "Yes, come." I hung up. The doctor took my phone, and they quickly wheeled me down the hall. My mind whirled in a confused state. I was concerned that my healthcare would expire, and I would not have coverage for the three weeks. Should I tell the doctor now or later?

CHAPTER 15
INTERRUPTION: I WANT TO LIVE

"THE OPERATING ROOM IS NOT AVAILABLE, and we have to perform her surgery now!" an unidentified person said.

"We have to prep this emergency room. Which process are we going to follow?" another voice said.

"Who's going to take the lead? The OR room or us, the ER team?" a female asked.

"I don't know, what do you think?" yet another female inquired.

"Who is going to make that decision?" a male asked.

My eyes opened, and I realized that the voices were coming from two people standing in front of me at the sink, washing their hands and talking about me.

"Excuse me Doc, I can hear you, but I have a request: Whatever you all do today, I cannot die," I said. "Today is my son's birthday. He was murdered a year ago, and I cannot die on his birth date; it would destroy my daughter."

I watched them look at each other, seemingly confused. One offered condolences, saying, "I'm sorry," and they kept scrubbing their hands.

A white-coated doctor came over to me and explained the procedure. During the process, my family was coming into the room in groups of two. Marcel and his girlfriend Paris, Damar and his girlfriend, Michelle, and Jackie stood around my ER bed. I could tell that they had all been crying; their eyes were red and puffy. My daughter stood in the background with her head down, listening as others were coming into the room.

Holding back tears and forcing a smile, Damar said, "If you pull through this, mom, I promise to go to church with you every week." He kept making more promises.

Marcel interrupted Damar's last promise and blurted out, "I'm not making those promises; just pull through the surgery."

As the group, except for Jackie, left the room, others entered. I assumed I was dying, and this was their opportunity to say goodbye. No one said the words, but their facial expressions and teary eyes made it obvious. I was too heavily sedated to move around or ask questions. Soon Jackie and I were in the room alone with the nurse. Jackie was trying hard to hold back her tears, but I knew this was it. She was saying goodbye, and we would never see each other again. With all the energy left in my body, I said to Jackie, "Please remember to pay my bills, go to work and take care of our house."

She leaned over, kissed me on the forehead, and said, "I love you, mom."

I overheard the nurses saying the waiting room was overcrowded. The doctor came in and gave me a detailed description of what was about to happen. He told me I had suffered an aneurysm, which meant a blood vessel burst, and I was bleeding in my brain. He would make an incision in my groin and insert a scope up to my brain to drain the blood. After the surgery, I would be in a medically induced coma for three weeks. He described it as a deep state of unconsciousness. The medicine given to me would cause a total lack of feeling, awareness, and potential memory loss, but it was necessary to protect my brain from swelling after the surgery. My family could talk to me, but I would not be able to respond to them.

I heard a man praying but was unable to detect which pastor it was. He had a deep voice, and his words of love and hope came across loud and clear. The other voices around me sounded muffled and distant. I recognized Alonzo's voice. His was a voice I had heard since I was 16 years old. I secretly called him my "WHY" guy. Why didn't we ever date? Why didn't we kiss? Why didn't we ever get married? But my WHY guy was here, and I was too medicated to talk. The voices seemed faint, but I could feel the presence of people. If anyone had whispered into my ear, "It's OK, let go and rest," I could have.

At some point, the room seemed brighter, but I could not visualize any faces. I only heard voices and the shuffling of people moving around in the room.

Beep . . . Beep . . . Beep was all I heard. How long had it been? Was I still in the hospital? Did I die and go to heaven? Beep . . . Beep . . . Beep was the only sound in the room.

I knew I wanted to live. Unable to carry this pain and fight for my life, something needed to change immediately. I remembered asking God to take me away. The pain of losing my son was too much to bear. Now I wanted to live. I began bargaining with God to save my life. I could feel the presence of a holy spirit; was it Jesus suspended over my bedside? Was He waiting for my soul to die and take me to heaven? Repeatedly, I said, "God, my son is dead, I am alive, and I want to live." Jesus never reached down to lift the pain from my body or take my soul. So, if Jesus needed something to take, He should carry this pain so I could fight for my life.

Reaching down in my soul, I lifted the weight of the grief and pain and gave it to Him. And in giving away all the pain and grief, I instantly felt the weight lifted off my heart. Jesus ascended away, and I continued my chant, "My son is dead, I am alive, and I want to live." As I repeated my petition, I dozed off to sleep.

I awakened with the nurse coming into the room to administer more meds. I wondered whether I survived surgery or was still waiting in the emergency room. How did I get to Boston? Why are Angel and Robin talking about me as if I am not in the room? How come I cannot respond? This time, I was able to hear what people were saying clearly. I heard Sarah's voice but could not see her. Someone asked me a question, but I was unable to respond. They gave me a pad and a pen. Whatever I wrote, I could hear the voice of Checkbox laughing; she was in the room. Soon I was able to distinguish the voices of Angel, Robin, and Jackie. Still unable to see them, I felt their presence. I don't remember the time of day, but it was dark every time I woke and looked out the window. My vision was blurry, but I could see Angel was sleeping in the chair. When I asked where Robin was, she said, "Sleeping in the waiting room. Only one person is allowed in the room at a time."

I was initially unaware of the medical bag next to my bed draining the blood from my head or the other large equipment and hoses attached to my body. But something was compelling me to get out of bed and get ready for work.

"I need to get dressed for work," I told Angel when she asked what I was doing.

Angel told me I wasn't going to work.

"If you are going to be my friend, you are not going to keep bossing me around and telling me what to do," I replied. "Why can't I go to work?"

"It's 1 a.m. Saturday," she said.

"OK, I don't work on weekends," I said and sunk back into the bed.

The nurse came into the room to adjust my head and encouraged me to stop moving. Apparently, every time I moved, it slowed down the blood draining from my head. She must have increased the dose of the medications that kept me sedated because I stopped shifting and dozed off into another weird dream.

I would periodically wake up and make a senseless comment. Whoever was in the room kept saying, "What are you talking about? Go back to sleep."

Every doctor who visited checked the left side of my body, telling me: "squeeze my hand," "move your left foot," or "can you feel this?"

I don't remember my responses, but they asked me the same questions at least three different times and left the room.

I attempted to get out of bed again for work, as I heard Angel say, "You are in the hospital; stop moving."

I replied, "Oh, I can't return to work without a doctor's note if it's been longer than three days."

The concept of time was vague. In my head, I left the hospital every night after the last visitor and returned in the morning. I thought

I was driving from Boston and traveling back to the hospital. Riding on the elevator and finding my room, I would undress, put on that hospital gown, and crawl back into the hospital bed.

The nurse came in and asked me the date and the name of the current president? I complained to the nurse that I could not determine day from night and had no clue what day it was. I asked her to raise the shade in the room so that I could detect day from night, and she obliged. Then I suggested she write the date on the board in front of my bed. This way, I could read the date.

My body and mind were fighting to re-engage in my environment. People were coming to visit me, but I didn't remember them or the conversations we had.

The nurse must have reduced my medication because eventually, I could determine day from night, the current date, and the name of the President—President Obama.

I barely remembered Angel and Robin telling me they were leaving to return home and would check on me later. They informed me that I was getting better.

"Better from . . .?" I thought.

I still didn't know what happened. The next thing I knew, Nichelle and Tanya were in my hospital room. Nichelle grabbed the blanket and said she was sleeping in the chair. She told me to get some rest. With the blinds open, I could determine that it was daytime. I did not remember how long I had been in the hospital, but it was daylight.

Someone said Darsweil was coming into town. His train arrived at 3 p.m. at Union Station, and someone needed to pick him up. It was the only thing people seemed to be saying. From my memory, Darsweil lived in North Carolina, and I wondered why he was on a train coming to Connecticut.

During Nichelle's visit, I asked, "Am I going to die?"

"No," she replied with a sigh and laughed.

Once Darsweil arrived, he told everyone to take the night off, and he slept in the same chair others had occupied. This six foot tall, Black man sat in the chair and looked uncomfortable, but he stayed. How I loved my cousin! He tried to engage me in a conversation about the bible. Unfortunately, I couldn't remember anything. Who were these people named King David and Peter the disciple that he continued to reference? Trying to hide my confusion, I asked if we could talk later and if he would remind me of this conversation. I also asked him if I was going to die.

"Is that why you are here?" I asked.

His firm, resounding "No!" gave me comfort, and I fell asleep. I don't remember how long he stayed, but no one else slept in the chair after he left. It must have been a lovely day because Darsweil was looking forward to walking to the train station.

Thanksgiving came, and I was still in the ICU. The day after, my physical therapist came and began walking me around the unit every day. He encouraged me to try walking three times a day to gain my strength and balance. What should have been a two-minute walk took 25 minutes. Soon the time it took me to walk the area shortened to 20 minutes, then 15 minutes, and 10 minutes was the fastest I could complete on my own. The physical therapist allowed me to sit in the chair. Yeah! And now I could eat solid food. My cousin Kim came by every day and put lotion on my feet. She knew I was concerned about my feet being dry.

Kim and I would talk about family and what was going on with everyone. However, every time I mentioned a particular person's name, the nurse came running into the room with a nervous look. She reported that my blood pressure was rising. We laughed as the nurse left the room. Then we did it again. I mentioned the family person's name, and the nurse again came running back into the room. This time she was annoyed and asked us to change the topic. Each time she recorded a rise in my blood pressure delayed my release date.

The pastor from Christian Tabernacle Baptist Church came for a short visit. I wondered if seeing me in this condition was too surreal. Bishop Brooks came by another day and prayed. He stood at the end of the bed and said, "I want you out of here in four days—four days," he repeated. Based on the date on the board in my room, I had to be out by December 3. Unsure what that meant or why he was so adamant about four days, I sat up in the bed. After Bishop Brooks left,

I increased the amount of time walking around the unit and pushed myself harder and longer in physical therapy.

On December 1, I moved out of ICU into a private room down the hall. One night, a member from the Old Testament Sunday School Class at Mount Aery Church arrived and gave me a Time Magazine with an article about Biblical Women. He didn't stay but encouraged me to get better and return to class soon. The following night, Dr. Edward and his wife came to visit. He informed me this was his second visit; I was sedated and kept mumbling about my son on the first visit. He was very pleased with my progress and reminded me to follow the doctor's orders once released. On December 3, the doctor came by and discussed my release date.

"I would discharge you today, but your blood pressure had erratic spikes, and we want to monitor you another day. If all goes well, we will release you on December 4," he said.

True to his word, the next day, I was sent home with a prescription to pick up and instructions to contact my primary doctor to remove stitches from my head in two weeks.

THE PRAYER BLANKET

The first thing I noticed when I arrived home was that the house was clean. Someone dusted, mopped, and shined my hardwood floors. When I looked in the kitchen, there were no dishes in the sink. Opening the refrigerator, I noticed it was clean and restocked with fresh items. When I looked at Jackie, she said, "Tanya and Nichelle did this. They didn't want you coming home to a dirty house." I phoned them to say thank you.

After telling Nichelle about my hospital discharge and expressing my appreciation, she said: "I have one question. What is yellow ketchup? I was feeding your granddaughter a hot dog, and she asked for yellow ketchup. Because I was in your house, I went looking for it, and when I could not find it, I had to tell her we were out."

I laughed and said, "Nichelle, there isn't any yellow ketchup. To convince her to eat mustard, I called it yellow ketchup. Now she likes mustard, but I forgot to tell her the real name." We both laughed.

She also told me she and Jackie logged into my bank account and paid certain bills, and I could rest easy.

Soror Jamaica came by and delivered a prayer blanket from Christian Tabernacle Baptist Church. The pastor wanted me to have it my first night home. She was only allowed to stay 10 minutes before Jackie gave her "the look" and thanked her for coming. Since when did my friends listen to my daughter? I was the grown-up. Jackie instructed me to go to bed. What normally would have been a 30-second, 12-step climb to my bedroom took me 10 minutes. Finally, I undressed and looked at my bed. I felt the same fear from months ago. Crawling into bed, I felt as if I would die if I went to sleep. I was afraid to ask my daughter or call Angel and ask if the doctor told them something about my health they had not shared. The only person I could talk to was God. Hesitantly, I pulled the prayer blanket over my body. I began chanting my prayer again, "God, my son is dead, I am alive, and I want to live." I took my pain medication, and as I was fighting the sleep out of fear, I saw a vision of an angel suspended over the left side of my body; she was pushing something out of my left side. I felt comforted and dozed off. The next morning, I was refreshed and less afraid. However, whenever taking a nap or retiring for the evening, I slept with the prayer blanket over my body.

JACKIE'S IN CHARGE

The following day, I received a call from Dr. Hadar checking on me.

"I know you can't talk long, but I wanted you to know that Checkbox called me and told me you had an aneurysm," Dr. Hadar said. "I thought the next words out of her mouth would be that you died. Instead, she said you were released from the hospital and were home recovering. I needed to tell you that you didn't have to do this for me to believe in your God."

I smiled and said, "Thank you."

Jackie was hovering again and made me hang up the phone. Later that day, I received another call from a coworker confirming that although my health insurance was due to expire, the new company had agreed to retain my contract and provide health insurance.

Regrettably, I needed to refill my prescriptions and have my doctor remove the stitches from my head in a week. How could I tell her that my eyesight was failing, and my doctors instructed me to stay off the computer? I called Checkbox for help, which was the best decision I made. She obtained all my medical forms and came to the house to get my signature.

Dr. Edward called and advised me to come to his office to have the stitches removed. He also assured me that despite my insurance issues, if I needed any medical attention, I should not hesitate to call him.

After the appointment to remove the stitches, Dr. Edward instructed me to go straight home and avoid the stores during the holidays. He cautioned me that the noise and stimulation would be exhausting and painful.

My daily routine was simple: shower, put on Jonathan's black sweatpants and socks, walk downstairs, eat a bowl of oatmeal, drink a cup of coffee, climb the stairs, and go to sleep. This activity left me mentally exhausted. When Jackie left for work, she texted me eight times a day in addition to calling my cellphone. If I didn't answer, she would have Angel or Sarah call to make sure I was alright. Sometimes, I was asleep or away from my phone. By the time I remembered where I had placed the cell or could get to it, whoever was calling hung up. One day I had eight missed calls and 20 anxious text messages asking where I was. But no matter how much I complained, the calls and texts did not subside. Jackie was in charge and seemingly enjoying it too much for my taste.

The following week, soror Hospitality called and informed me she spoke to my daughter and arranged for my sorors to bring us dinner every night. My daughter instructed them only to stay three to five minutes with minimal talking. She gave soror Hospitality a list of foods we enjoyed eating. Soror Hospitality agreed to coordinate every visit through my daughter. Jackie was now the mother and caretaker. It was great to have her around but also personally humiliating. She even went to my Facebook page and warned people to stop calling, texting, or coming by the house because I needed my rest. They listened.

I was so grateful for the food because I was too weak to cook and didn't remember how to prepare meals anymore. It was a painful reality that the culinary professional, my mother's daughter, did not know how to season or cook food. Nichelle and Tanya offered to send food via Stop and Shop Pod.

I noticed my daughter hovering over me, and when I fell asleep, she checked to see if I was still breathing. It was becoming irritating. One day, I sat in the living room and waited for her to wake up. I wanted to know why she was hovering and why all the increased text messages from people asking if I was alright. I wanted to know what was really going on. Jackie realized that it was time for an explanation.

WHAT HAD HAPPENED WAS . . .

"The doctor at the hospital informed me that your chances of surviving the surgery were not promising," Jackie said, sitting across from me in the living room. "He said the aneurysm did extensive damage and that you had been bleeding in your brain for the past 24 hours. The left side of your body had already begun to shut down.

"I asked him to explain his diagnosis to my aunts," she continued. "I was scared and didn't know what to do, so I did a three-way call with Auntie Angel and Nichelle. Angel and Robin were on the highway driving from Boston in the pouring rain and Nichelle was sitting at her office desk in Maryland. I merged the calls, and the neurosurgeon informed them that you were likely not going to survive the surgery and that they should consider plans for your funeral. The phone was silent on both ends. Auntie Angel said she was one hour away and Nichelle said, 'Have faith. She will be there tomorrow.'

"Hanging up, I walked into the waiting room and informed every one of the news from the doctor. I asked them to pray," Jackie continued, agonized as she recalled the events. "Soror Fitness and all the others posted on social media asking everyone to pray for soror Cooper. I called Rev. Lammie and shared the doctor's prognosis. Rev. Lammie called Bishop Watts and asked for prayers. She sent out text messages and emails asking for prayers for Professor Cooper. Everyone who received the text or email began praying and sending it to people in their contacts. Everyone connected to someone in their network began praying. Soror Social Media posted the information on her wall, and others began calling your cellphone. Because you volunteered to work as the second project manager with soror Cowboys, she sent an email to the Eastern Region Conference planning team and your chapter president sent out an email asking every one of them for immediate prayers for soror Cooper."

Jackie concluded, "Mom, we had everyone and every organization you were connected to praying. Your cellphone was receiving calls and texts of prayers day and night. And by the way, you had too many appointment reminders and tasks to complete. I deleted them permanently from your phone. The surgery lasted for hours, and I was scared."

She began crying as she retold the story.

"After the surgery, the doctor lowered the anesthesia, and your body started to respond. Therefore, they didn't need to place you in an induced coma. However, the left side of your body did not respond, and they informed me that you would be paralyzed after the surgery. The neurosurgeon said some patients tend to die days or within three months after surgery," she said, sniffing.

"Your sorors Fitness, Raydio and others were in the waiting room when the family returned, expecting to hear that you died. When they walked through the ER doors, soror Fitness told them, 'Change your faces; she is alive. God is present, and our prayers have been answered.'"

Jackie explained that she had not been able to sleep, knowing I could die within the next three months. That is why she had been hovering, and people were constantly checking on my recovery. My daughter begged me to follow the doctor's orders and please rest.

"You have survived a brain aneurysm and need to continue healing," she said.

Before she got up from the couch, she took a deep breath and said the doctors also warned her I could have a second aneurysm but that they would continue monitoring me.

"Momma, please don't resume your same activities. Your brain can't handle it," she said. Then her voice lowered when she added,

"Mom, while they were preparing you for surgery, you told me to go to work and don't forget to pay your bills. I was so worried about you; I could not work. When I got to work, I had an emotional breakdown in the kitchen, and they sent me home."

Taking a deep breath, I apologized.

"I have been conditioned to work and pay bills and I passed that same traumatic family expectation to you," I said. "Next time something happens to me, do not do as I said."

With tears running down her face, she kissed me on my forehead.

When I thought she was finished, she took another deep breath and said while I was in the hospital the daycare called regarding Maya suddenly misbehaving. She was hitting other children, withdrew from classroom activities, and would not listen to the teachers. Her typical school day ended at 5 p.m., but Jackie had to leave work early and pick her up every day at noon.

I quickly understood that Maya had been traumatized at such an early age. And my granddaughter had been unable to verbally express her pain about the trauma of her Uncle Coop's death, my abrupt physical absence from the house, and the health problems of her other grandmother, who was also in the hospital. Maya's routine had drastically changed, and the people she spent time with were disappearing. Her mother was stressed and alone. Placing my arms around Jackie, I told her we would handle this together.

The next day Jackie and I met with the director and staff at the daycare to discuss our many traumas in the last two years. They appreciated the information and recommended we try to spend time with my granddaughter over the holidays to reacclimate her to a daily routine allowing her to feel more relaxed. I requested that all school records about Maya's behavior include comments about what four-year-old Maya was experiencing at home. The notes needed to state that my son was murdered by mistaken identity vs. gun violence to avoid the mischaracterization of a Black man being shot. The school personnel supported our request and were accommodating.

By Christmas, with both grandparents out of the hospital, a sense of comfort and normalcy returned. Maya's loving, charming behavior and attitude had returned after Christmas break.

MS. CLAUS IS COMING TO TOWN

Cindy and I had reconnected in recent years and were Facebook friends. She had read Jackie's Facebook postings and was concerned about her feeling overwhelmed and alone with the Christmas holiday approaching.

"Don't fuss, but I purchased a plane ticket and will be there tomorrow to help Jackie," Cindy said during a phone call.

I needed to accept her love and support. While Cindy was visiting, she drove me to get my hair cut to camouflage my balding blotches from the radiation used in surgery. Cindy also played Ms. Claus by placing gifts underneath the Christmas tree for Maya. Against my doctor's orders, we went to the store early in the day when they were less busy. It was still too much walking and talking. All I could do was point to certain clothes items or gifts and Cindy purchased them. Maya was excited about seeing the wrapped packages underneath the tree for her. Cindy played board games with Maya, checked on Jackie, and helped me sort through bills. She stayed for two weeks, bringing joy and love into the house. She stood in the gap for me!

Sorors called and dropped off gifts for Maya. Christmas was beginning to look hopeful. After Cindy left, Checkbox and I kept making phone calls to the office and repeatedly sent emails until I finally received the forms to apply for COBRA insurance. By mid-January, two months after being released from the hospital, I had insurance. And then my short-term disability was approved, and Jackie and I could breathe, buy food, and pay bills.

Jackie was not really excited about celebrating her birthday, so I ordered a few pizzas, a cake from the bakery, and called her friends and family. Regardless of what I was feeling, we celebrated our birthdays. I mustered up the spirit of my mother and pulled something fun together for Jackie. Although I spent most of the time upstairs in my room, I enjoyed hearing the laughter.

HARDHEADED

As time went on, it became increasingly difficult for me to remain idle. What did rest really mean? I couldn't read a book. The mental stimulation was overwhelming. I couldn't remember the content from the previous chapter. So, I tried listening to the bible on tape; that too was exhausting. My mind would shut down and not listen or remember what I just heard. The television was worse than reading. Dr. Edward warned me about trying to resume my life activities too soon. The cost of my disobedience was severe and painful. Tired of sitting in the house every day, I asked Nichelle and Tanya if I could ride the train to visit them. They both said no. Stay home and rest.

"You are the only one who hasn't realized that you had brain surgery," Nichelle said. "The constant motion from the train is going to be overwhelming and increase your mental confusion and memory loss, and it could kill you."

So, I listened and stayed home.

Being hardheaded, in March, I convinced Angel and Robin to let me come to Boston on the train. I set alarms on my watch as reminders to get off the train, walk downstairs, and call to confirm my arrival. With all these preparations and reminders, I was still confused. I got off the train and was in an unfamiliar environment. The train station seemed hazy, my vision was blurry, and my left eye could barely focus. Finally, regaining my awareness, I found the Uber I reserved waiting for me outside the station. Soon, Four the Hard Way was back together again, eating dinner.

In all our years of friendship and hanging out, I was never the silent one. After dinner, we rode to Robin's house as we had done in previous years, talking, laughing, and reminiscing about life. When the room grew quiet, Cindy looked at me concerned.

"What's wrong? You are not talking or laughing?" she asked.

Fighting back the tears and pain in my head, I replied, "Just listening."

Ten minutes later, we drove to Angel's house, where I took pain medication and began sobbing uncontrollably. My nerves felt like someone was playing Double-Dutch with my veins; with every turn of the rope, my body ached. Angel gave me some Tylenol and told me to stay in bed. The train ride and interacting with my friends were overwhelming. Doctor E was correct. My disobedience had painful consequences.

I stayed in bed for two days recovering and dreading the train ride home, which was just as painful. When I arrived home, Jackie took my bag to my bedroom and watched me crawl into the bed. There I stayed for another week, and I promised myself to behave in the future.

VEGAN LIFESTYLE

Although I was able to stand for more extended periods, my memory was still horrible. On a few occasions, I burned meat and nearly started a kitchen fire. Jackie was becoming increasingly concerned about the house and my safety. She offered to cook my meat and leave it in the refrigerator. Although her suggestion made good logical sense, it made me feel like an aging person. And I wasn't going to eat microwaved meat.

"Sweetheart, my mother was a chef and I have dined at 5-star restaurants all my life. I have experienced some of the best international chefs in Europe. Eating microwave food is not something I could ever do," I said, standing in the middle of the kitchen floor with my hands on my hips.

Not pleased with my response, Jackie threatened to call the aunties for reinforcement. Unmoved by her challenge, I compromised and offered to become a vegan rather than eating microwaved food. Jackie looked at me as if I had lost my mind. Asking what I knew about being a vegan, she laughed because she knew how much I loved a steak.

I went to Facebook seeking information about becoming a vegan. The next thing I knew, a former coworker who had moved to North Carolina responded with links to various sites while other friends emailed me vegan recipes. Sorors sent emails and more links for me to follow. The following week, I received two cookbooks from North Carolina on eating vegan. It was going so well that soror Social Media invited me to have a vegan dinner at a local restaurant. It was a six-course meal accompanied by a different wine for every course.

"If I could only learn to cook like this, I would never eat meat again," I said, while sitting in the restaurant feeling regal.

CHAPTER 16
INTERRUPTION: REINVENTING MYSELF

AS A VEGAN, FRIED CHICKEN WAS not in my new meal plan. However, the smell remained tempting, and Jackie intentionally left the dark meat on the counter to torture me. My son would have been home playing his stupid rap music with his friends, who would also be there to eat dinner. Jackie and I were adjusting to the quiet, although it seemed life had left the house. We sat at the dinner table, making small talk, and avoiding talking about how we missed Jonathan. We were trying to adjust to our new normal—another year without Jonathan. After dinner, I retired to my room early and cried myself to sleep. I awoke to a text from Jackie saying she had gone out and would return later.

"Don't worry, mom, I will be safe," her text message said.

Apparently, my anxiety over Jackie's safety had become excessive. It became easier for her to send a text rather than talking and assuring me she would be safe.

Jackie decided to take a mini vacation to Virginia and spend time with family. Maya stayed with her other grandmother, leaving me home alone.

Arriving home to an empty house, I quickly remembered that Damar asked if I could officiate his wedding, which they wanted to have at the house where they spent most of their teenage and young adult years. Tomorrow was enough time to pick up a cake and a bottle of champagne for the occasion. Marcel was the best man, and Paris was the photographer.

It was a wonderful moment to have them experience an adult

transition. We placed a picture of Coop on the mantel to have him included in the ceremony. My spirits were high, but I was mentally exhausted afterward. It would have been wiser to have someone else officiate the wedding, but I needed to marry Damar, who was like my son. He and Marcel were dedicated to standing in the gap for their best friend and brother Coop. I needed to say the words and feel the role of a mother watching her son get married. After the joy and laughter left the house, the quiet returned as a reminder.

GOOGLE IT

The house was too quiet and I was bored. I began looking on the Internet for people I lost contact with over the years. Every night for hours, I explored all the social media sites and googled a different name. Three weeks into searching, I found a few people. Sometimes, I would call Angel and ask her if I liked the old boyfriends before making contact. The laughter and memories were good for the soul. However, the best discovery was my line sister, my ace, the first person standing in the line of six. I was her deuce, the second in line after ace. Dr. Joy Ohayio answered my Facebook request and called me. We screamed with joy over reconnecting.

We sounded like hens cackling on the farm. Joy still resided in New Jersey. We laughed and reminisced for hours on the phone and promised to meet in New York once the weather got warm. It had been 30 years since we last saw one another. The first five minutes, we caught up. Yes, she was still married; no, I was divorced. Kids, yes, we both had two. I wondered when a mother stops saying that her child is dead. However, I was not ready to stop, so I began with my standard line, "My son was murdered by mistaken identity, and I had a brain aneurysm a year later on his birthdate." That conversation is still painful to repeat and always changes the mood of the conversation. Joy and I scheduled our next conversation for May, the month we crossed over into Delta Sigma Theta Sorority, Inc.

GRACE AND MERCY

I will never forget March 15, 2018, the day I realized the miracle happening in my life. Although I worked my entire adult life, I had never been able to pay all my bills by the 15th of the month and have a fully stocked refrigerator. As I opened the bills on my desk, they all showed no payment was due that month, a first in my adult life. The next payment was due in April 2018. I knew it was the grace and mercy of God. All I needed to do now was go upstairs and follow my doctors' orders and rest. On this day, I released my anger toward God and accepted that He did save my son. He saved his soul. It was people, who made a bad choice, who killed my son—not God.

My friend Jazz called and said she was picking me up to eat seafood. I proudly informed Jazz that I was now a vegan and didn't eat meat. She laughed and came anyway. I sat at the restaurant watching her devour the shrimp and scallops and remembered Dr. Edward saying, "Please do not punish yourself. If you want to eat meat, eat it." I thought about New Year's Eve when Jackie ate all the fried chicken and kept licking her fingers. I decided, "You have been through enough," and caved in. A woman sitting next to us overheard our conversation and told me that she had the same problem with giving up seafood, so she became a pescatarian. I forgot what a pescatarian was, so I googled it. When I read I could eat seafood and regular cheese, I began to smile. That day I relinquished being a vegan and became a pescatarian.

"I knew that wasn't going to last long," Jazz said and laughed when I told her about the change.

Jazz suggested I grow herbs in a garden to complement my healthy eating plan and to keep me occupied during the day. We went to the store and purchased pots of mint, basil, peppers, oregano, and thyme. YouTube became my best friend to teach me how to garden, and my friends on Facebook responded to all my beginner questions. This new adventure was great! I taught my granddaughter how to care for the garden, and we had a new project together.

While I was gardening one day, Marcel and Paris came to visit and to tell me they were engaged and planning their wedding for next year. They asked me to officiate the wedding. I felt proud and sad simultaneously; tears came rolling down my face—tears of joy and happiness, but also tears of sorrow. It seemed everyone was moving forward in their lives except me. Events like these were when I missed my son the most and became angry about my restrictions.

The men that murdered my son stole more than his life. Coop had dreams. I remember asking for seven grandchildren between him and Jackie. Now I am borrowing the dreams of his friends to fill my void. I was thankful that Marcel and Damar still included me in their lives—a blessing. It would be my joy to perform Marcel and Paris' ceremony. My days continued with little to do but water the garden and watch the vegetables grow. Jazz had to return for more tutorials on pulling the leaves of the herb garden.

One day I noticed I had several missed phone calls from my cousin Sunshine in Florida. When I finally returned her calls, she reminded me of the next family reunion the following month. She had a last-minute cancellation, and with the cruise not honoring refunds, she offered me the room. Thanking her, I declined because of financial restrictions.

"I know, but I got you!" she immediately responded.

"YES! I accept," I said, but had to explain my health limitations because of the brain aneurysm.

The cruise was great, and my family was extremely accommodating of my limitations. The weather and food were perfect, and I had a chance to bond with Nikki, Sunshine's daughter. Nikki announced she was engaged and getting married in Portland, Oregon, after completing her master's degree program. I offered to officiate the wedding if she could not find a minister in her area. Officiating Nikki's wedding would be my first same-gender wedding, and it would be an honor to give back to cousin Sunshine.

After the cruise, I spent another week in Bradenton, Florida, with friends who served in ministry at my church in Bridgeport. In exchange for the hospitality, I cooked dinner every night for the family. While there, I also reconnected with other family members whom I had not seen in over 40 years. My cousin Gloria, living in Tampa, drove down and took me out for crab, a family tradition. She tried hard not to dwell on my facial expressions and noticed the constant rubbing of my head. When I became over stimulated, the location where the doctors made an incision in my head began throbbing, which meant I was fatigued.

"Look at God!" I said, despite feeling the pain.

I had been working since I was 16 years old and had never been able to afford a weeklong cruise to the Bahamas and a second week in Florida. Wow! After my vacation, I boarded the plane and began pondering how I was going to live out my life with all my health and personal challenges.

GRAMMAR FOR DUMMIES

My friend Jazz, after noticing my text messages were difficult to read, suggested that I contact the Communication Disorder Department at Southern Connecticut State University. They offered services at no cost to individuals who had difficulties communicating because of disorders resulting from strokes and brain injuries. My first visit was horrible. The team gave me a simple assignment to read the instructions of tasks, prioritizing them on the sheet of paper. As a project manager, this was going to be easy until I started reading. I could not read two sentences before my head started throbbing. I didn't understand the instructions and what seemed easy took me an hour before I threw down the pencil and gave in. While her staff encouraged me not to be too hard on myself, the director of the program scheduled me to return in the fall for hour-long sessions once a week.

"Based on your injury, be thankful that you can still read and write," a department staff member said.

The aneurysm had damaged my brain, and I had to relearn the basic skills of communication. My pride was wounded, and I started yelling at God again.

"Why make me acquire student loan debt to graduate from Howard University, work as an adjunct professor and earn a master's degree if only to bring me here, incapable of reading and writing?" I asked. "That does not make any sense to me."

Nonetheless, I kept my weekly appointments and every semester I began to show progress. I asked soror Raydio to provide private tutoring. We purchased two books, including Grammar for Dummies, and she assigned me additional homework. I tried to stay positive, but it was humiliating and hard. I also met with Dr. Edward every three months for the first year after the aneurysm.

ANCIENT CHINESE SECRET

During a visit, Dr. Edward noticed I was walking slower and holding onto the walls to turn corners. He suggested I join Aiping Tai Chi in Orange, Connecticut, to improve my balance and help me regain my self-confidence. Once again, I asked, "Doc, when can I return to work?" Looking up from his laptop, he gave his standard response after every appointment, which was no response.

I followed his orders and joined Aiping Tai Chi and soon was addicted to the classes. For one hour a day, my mind was emptied and rejuvenated. It took me awhile to learn the movements and avoid looking like a robot, but I stayed with it. My sleep pattern improved, and I became less irritable about my restrictions.

Still unable to read for longer than 20 minutes before getting a headache, I downloaded the Bible.IS app, which read the scriptures to me. Every aspect of my life had to change, and I was determined to search for new ways to feel relevant. Although my writing had shown some improvement, reading continued to be difficult. Every day, I reread what I wrote the previous day, and it did not make sense. What the heck was I talking about? I could not write a sentence with clarity and struggled to remember how to convert a singular to plural noun. However, I kept trying.

After several missed calls, my soror Fitness called again to check in. Moments into our conversation here came another recommendation from her. Another person telling me what I should do. Soror Fitness suggested I come to her gym, called Ful-Fit Fitness in West Haven, where I could work out with the owner, Rob, who would help improve my fitness. At this point, I was overwhelmed by all the suggestions. I had enough help, I thought. There was someone to help with balance, another someone to help with grammar, and someone to help heal my wounded heart and head. Soror Fitness, however, would not accept my "No thanks, I'm good." She insisted I go to the gym and sent Rob a text. We met the following day, and once again I explained my medical history and admitted I had not exercised my body in over a year because of the brain aneurysm. During the conversation, tears began rolling down my face as my body tensed from retelling my sad story over again.

"Rob, I'm sorry for crying, but I have had enough," I apologized.

"No worries. I will see you tomorrow," he said, smiling.

Rob suggested I work out with him four times a week and follow the strict meal plan he recommended. After two months I could only lift 7 pounds and couldn't run on the treadmill at all. My financial situation became an issue in my effort to continue to pursue fitness training. I shifted my money from the tai chi class to pay Rob, but that was not enough. I could not afford any additional sessions even though I could feel the difference in my limbs. Rob projected I needed another year to best recover.

"Do you trust God?" Rob asked, in response to my financial worries.

"Of course," I replied.

"Then keep working," he yelled. "You can't afford to quit. Your body needs the exercise and you have lots of people in your corner who love you. I made some phone calls, so keep praying and moving."

I trusted God and continued the painful workouts. My lack of mobility over the past year contributed to the pain. Rob was patient and asked me to be the same. I remained committed to both fitness and the communications sessions, praying God had a plan for all this humiliation. I lost 10 pounds and posted the news on FB.

VIP TICKETS

My friend KimBianca called to congratulate me on the weight loss and asked if I wanted to join her for a night out at the MGM Springfield Casino with VIP Tickets. It was an opportunity to dress up and be a grown-up for the night. KimBianca had to drive my car, and we stayed overnight in Springfield. I pulled out my sexiest red evening gown and high heels. Walking into the casino was magical. The staff welcomed KimBianca and me, rolling out the red carpet.

"The entire floor is yours, no money needed. Eat and drink whatever you desire," the hostess said.

From that point, I lost my mind, dismissing all of Jackie's advice about drinking. For this once-in-a-lifetime event, I was drinking champagne all night. I was willing to pay the price of being over-exerted and physically exhausted when I returned home. But tonight, Odell was back and going to enjoy every moment. KimBianca and I stayed up until 2 a.m. talking, eating and roaming the new casino.

Once I returned home, I was confined to my bedroom for a week. The constant throbbing in my head was painful. Every vein rattled like chimes, but it was worth it.

Concerned about my health, KimBianca called to check in. She could hear the pain and joy in my voice.

"O, I am not trying to get in trouble with Jackie or make you sicker, but I have floor tickets for the Stevie Wonder concert in two weeks. Would you like to go with me?" she asked, with a slight hesitation.

"Yes, Yes, Yes. I will stay in bed and be rested by then," I said, enthusiastically accepting the invitation. "Thank you."

Jackie was frustrated with my decisions and lack of control in following the doctors' orders. Although I knew the loud music and lights would be excruciating, it was Stevie Wonder! We had floor seats. KimBianca drove again. I made my way to the front row and enjoyed the evening. Although Stevie performed, he too was grieving a personal loss. "The Queen," Aretha Franklin, was buried two days before this concert, and his spirits were low, but he sang and honored her in his grief. Once again; I returned home and needed two weeks to recover from being overstimulated. I could sense Jackie becoming annoyed with my constant excuses about why I laid in bed all week in pain. I told her, "It was Stevie Wonder!"

My cousin Nikki phoned and asked if I could still officiate her wedding in May 2019 in Portland, Oregon. Nikki and her fiancé, Mimi, planned to have their wedding ceremony conducted on the mountainside at a winery. I was proud to assist my cousin Sunshine in providing her daughter with a memorable ceremony. Jackie was not pleased with my behavior and began reporting my carelessness to her aunties.

DALLAS COWBOYS

The following month Paris and Marcel had their bridal brunch, which Jackie and I attended, allowing us to meet both families. It was clear I had not spent any quality time with Paris. At the brunch, I met her father, who lived in Dallas, Texas. During our conversation, he mentioned he worked for the Dallas Cowboys football team franchise. I shared that I had been a fan since I was a child since the Roger Staubach and Coach Tom Landry days. I reflected on my early years when my brother-in-law Roger watched us while the women went shopping or cooking. A Cowboys fan, he didn't want us to interfere with him watching the games on television.

"The Cowboys are playing," he said. "If I have to yell at you from another room and miss a play, I'm going to beat your ass."

So, he made us sit in the room with him while he watched the game. We could not talk. I was 10 years old and forced to watch the Dallas Cowboys play, so I liked or disliked the same teams and players that Roger did.

Now, Paris' father was inviting me to the AT&T stadium to watch a home game. I thanked him and said I would coordinate something with Paris next season.

"Why wait, come next month," he said. "The Cowboys are playing the (Philadelphia) Eagles. It should be a great game."

I am not sure how it happened, but in November, Paris and I headed to Dallas for my first Cowboys home game. The stadium was awesome, and Paris' family provided VIP treatment. I watched the game in Jerry Jones' suite eating prawns and drinking wine. Jackie warned Paris to limit my drinking because, after one drink, I would get a pounding headache and be unable to function the next day. But I was in Dallas, Texas, watching the Cowboys play. Again, I reflected on how well God was treating me since my surgery. The trip was memorable, and I took plenty of pictures. Once I returned home, my recovery from all the excitement was longer, but it was worth it. I repeatedly told Jackie, "It was the Cowboys!" She strongly suggested I stop behaving like a child and take better care of myself.

November also was time to celebrate Coop's date of birth. I stopped calling it his birthday because it became too painful. Birthday celebrations are happy but November 15th was not. The night was emotionally painful, and I decided this was too depressing. I did not want to carry this sadness again. My mother had always celebrated my birthday and I was going to keep the tradition going at all costs. However, this time, I asked Jackie, Damar and Marcel permission to let go of planning and celebrating this day. They agreed, and we discussed another way to honor Coop without me being sad. Marcel said the 15th also was Paris' birthday and suggested they could celebrate me.

"Me? It's not my birthday," I replied.

"Mom, you asked God to give you a reason to love Nov. 15 again, and He did. He saved you on Coop's birthday," Jackie said. "God gave us a reason to love this day again. So, we will celebrate you and Paris."

Holding my daughter in my arms, I cried and thanked her.

The next day, like clockwork, the phantom delivered happy birthday balloons, candles, and a bouquet of flowers. I told Jackie that I was determined to find out who was leaving these gifts of love every year.

CHAPTER 17
INTERRUPTION: TURNING TRAUMA INTO HEALING

DURING AN APPOINTMENT WITH DR. EDWARD in January, my health was stable. He determined we didn't need to meet every three months. As I sat waiting in the exam room, I was praying he would release me from medical disability and approve my request to return to work. I was grateful that I survived the aneurysm, but I was feeling worthless. An unemployed Howard University graduate, a licensed minister, not allowed to preach, and my teaching assignment was reduced along with my salary. Because of the overstimulation concerns, my activities were limited. This could not be what God had planned for my life? I wanted my life back to the way it was before the aneurysm.

Dr. Edward came into the exam in his usual jovial style. Over the 20 years as his patient, he hadn't gained a pound and never looked disheveled. He was a good-looking White man from the Bronx, who wore nice shoes and had a sense of humor. He immediately detected I was troubled and instantly shifted into doctor mode. I began venting about my lack of patience with the last year and asked if I could return to work?

"Odell, it's time we have an honest conversation," he said firmly, with a stern look. "Every month, you have asked me this question, and I have casually dismissed providing you with an answer. Well, dear, here is the truth.

"The life you had before the aneurysm is gone. Last appointment, you complained about memory loss, confusion, and your need to use a GPS whenever you drove. Are you still having those problems?"

"Yes," I replied.

"Throughout this year, I've recommended that you not travel on the train or drive to Boston. You didn't listen and became sicker due to being overstimulated, and you spent days in bed recovering. Odell, THIS TIME I NEED YOU TO LISTEN!" he said, nearly shouting.

"I suggest you reinvent yourself. Seek something you enjoy doing that gives you pleasure and do it. I'm not saying your life is over, but it's time you accepted the second phase of your life must be different. You will never survive a full day in the workplace meeting the demands that would be expected of you."

Listening to him brought tears to my eyes. I knew he was right, but I didn't want to hear it. I started crying on the exam table.

"I am confident that you will find a way to reinvent yourself and be happy," he continued.

Tears ran down my face as I drove directly home, went to my room, and cried myself to sleep. Dr. Edward had been saying what he told me that day all along, but I wasn't listening.

The next day, I phoned the people who would encourage me and tell me what I wanted to hear, hoping they would give me another solution. Unfortunately, they all agreed with Dr. Edward and said someone finally told me the truth. Apparently, I was the only one who had not accepted that I had a brain aneurysm and almost died. Nichelle reminded me I was supposed to be paralyzed on my left side. Robin and Tanya asked if I had been able to read a book without getting a headache.

"You still have problems driving without getting lost," Angel said.

Everyone seemed relieved I was beginning to accept the truth of how my life needed to change, including Jackie. When I updated her the next day, she also didn't seem surprised by the diagnosis.

"Mom, I know you will figure something out," she said. "Now, will you rest and stop worrying about returning to work."

Still not convinced, I tried one more option. I called Nurse Betty. She started laughing during the phone call.

"I could have told you that," she said in her loving yet stern voice.

This was difficult to hear. I needed time to adapt.

Winter was approaching again. The thought of wearing Jonathan's black sweatpants and socks was depressing. Other than my fitness and tai-chi classes, I didn't have an outlet. I could feel myself sinking into a depression. I saw on Facebook that my graduating class of 1980 would celebrate its 40th-year high school reunion in 2020. I did not see anyone coordinating the reunion activities, so I sent a few Facebook posts to certain classmates who had been active in keeping the Tech Tiger spirit alive. By the end of December, I had successfully recruited 11 Tech alumni from the class of 1980 to join the reunion planning team. I promised to carry out most of the assignments since I was the only one unemployed. They agreed, and we began planning. When my classmates asked what I was doing now, again I said, "I am the mother of a murdered son and I suffered a brain aneurysm on his birth date and almost died." As always these words changed the mood of the conversation; people immediately began extending their condolences. All the logistics were confirmed before Christmas, and we agreed to halt planning until late February. Meanwhile, we needed to reclaim as many classmates as possible.

Class reunion planning went smoothly as spring approached. I felt good about getting outdoors again. Sitting in the yard, I noticed the Jehovah's Witness returned to visit. She was pleased to see that my attitude and love for God had returned. When she asked if I had returned to work, I searched for the words to respond. I was tired of my routine answer, "My son was murdered, and on his birth date, I suffered a brain aneurysm." Our visit was much better, and I thanked her for the prayers, constant visits and apologized for my rudeness.

"You were angry with God, but I knew He would heal your heart," she said, as she laughed.

The following day, I found myself sitting underneath my tree again when a text from my neighbor arrived reminding me about a fundraising event for a new mayoral candidate. I decided to attend but wanted to arrive late. While I was mingling with people, I recognized a friend I had not seen in years. I didn't know that he lived in New Haven. Jonathan Berryman was still an incredible musician and teacher in New Haven. He and I were standing with a group of people when someone asked me what I did for a living. This time, I had a better response. "I'm reinventing myself." Most of the people smiled and laughed.

I changed the topic to avoid any further questioning. Before I left the event, Berryman cornered me and wanted to know more about my response. He wanted me to explain what I meant by reinventing myself. Because we were Facebook friends and he knew about my son, I didn't have to provide all the details. But he wanted details of my healing. Before the conversation ended, Berryman suggested I share my story.

"People need to hear your story. You could help someone else on their journey," he said.

I was adamant about not having the aptitude for writing a play or book.

"But you know people who can," he replied.

Before we left the event, Berryman had convinced me to text a mutual acquaintance to explore ways to share my story.

In the next month, Berryman, Aleta, and Rev. Anderson were sitting at my kitchen table strategizing how to tell my story in a stage production and in book form. The four of us met for months afterward defining roles, partnerships, and resources. One of my strengths was that I was persistent and eager to learn. They coached me through the process of being a playwright. And I began networking and applying for grant funding. God sent me other coaches and mentors, who were experts in the fields of PTSD and mental health, to volunteer their time.

In the summer, Tim Raynor, now Dr. Raynor and the executive director of the School of Professional Studies at the University of Bridgeport, called and offered me an adjunct contract for the summer. The title of the course was The Pursuit of Happiness. I would be teaching from the book entitled Authentic Happiness by Martin E.P. Seligman, Ph.D. My challenge was to adapt my teaching style to this new topic and concept, and to deliver the curriculum flawlessly. I still had difficulty with my reading and writing skills. To compensate, I ordered an audiobook and highlighted the key points in the hard copy. The makeup of the class was 22 adult students from various backgrounds. Some had been in prison; others were veterans, working mothers and fathers, survivors from the Haiti earthquake, and wealthy students from Saudi Arabia, who had never worked a day in their lives. All had experienced some level of trauma in their lives.

On the first day, I explained the course outline and assignments. One student kept questioning me about the final project, which was blank on the outline because I had not decided how to end the course. During my explanation, I told the students that I wanted to teach them how to deal with the interruptions in their lives. We would utilize the information in the book and through discussions with each other to discover that there were lessons learned from their childhood, friendships, family, relationships, faith and educations to be resilient, and to rebound after a traumatic interruption.

While teaching the course, I realized God was teaching me the same lessons.

The eight weeks of class were outstanding. I was transparent and taught the class through my experience of being a mother of a murdered son, diagnosed with PTSD and suffering a brain aneurysm on his birth date, and being a minister in the Baptist Church. The students connected with my story and began opening up about their journeys and challenges. God used this to shape the beginning of my journey toward reinventing myself. I learned from the book, Authentic Happiness, that I, too, had all the qualities and abilities from my childhood, faith and relationships, and that I could learn to be happy. The challenge was selecting pieces from these aspects of my life to reinvent myself. I just had to adjust my attitude and perspective.

In September, my pastor, Dr. Bennett, announced he would ordain five ministers, including me. By the end of the month, I was Rev. O and feeling good about reinventing myself and my new journey. After the ordination, I had a brief conversation at the church with another associate minister.

"Congratulations, Rev. Odell!" she began. "I was thinking about our past conversations about God and you asking why God didn't save your son."

"You know God didn't save His son either," she continued. "He did save His soul."

"How could I forget something so obvious?" I replied. We laughed and hugged as we left the room.

I began feeling more optimistic about my life. November was approaching again, and Jackie and I were less anxious. This time, I was determined to catch the phantom. At last, I yelled, "Jackie, Jackie, come outside." The phantom was carrying balloons, candles, and a bouquet of flowers. It was Fresh, Jonathan's college classmate. Jonathan and Fresh met through their mutual love of making music. To my amazement, for the last four years, Fresh had been driving down from Enfield, twice a year to leave these gifts of love. I called Jackie outside, and we talked with her for an hour. I asked Fresh why she never left a note or card.

"It wasn't for you," she replied. "It was for Coop. He knew I was here."

Before the holidays began, Pastors Anderson, Berryman, Aleta, and I met to plan the calendar for 2020. I told the team that I had a name for the book and production. They all gave me a skeptical look.

"What is it?" one of them asked.

I told them the story about my class and then how I settled on the title. They immediately liked my suggestion and agreed that "Interruptions" would be the name. I was in awe and totally dependent on God directing my path. Celebrating my reinvention and the birth of Interruptions generated mixed emotions because it all began with my Coop's death. Now I have truly reinvented myself and help people through the traumatic interruptions in their lives.

A friend suggested I become a podcaster and continue sharing stories and offering healing on a different platform. Nervous about my abilities, I asked the team working with me at the Communication Center to review my notes and listen to my podcasts. It was important that I not sound boring or repetitive. My struggles were remembering information or using the correct vocabulary. The team listened and evaluated two of my shows and gave me the confidence I needed. Two years later I was released from my sessions at the communications disorder center. The team felt that I had made progress with the play production and podcasting, showing remarkable growth.

In the middle of launching the production, COVID 19 surfaced as a global pandemic, and the world had shut down, the theater disappeared. *Interruptions: Disrupting the Silence* shifted from a stage performance to online production.

The world learned that trauma did not disappear or subside from communities of color. The pandemic placed a spotlight on racial inequity and prejudices toward communities of color. *Interruptions: Disrupting the Silence* addressed the disparity and ongoing trauma in lives regardless of education, faith, or zip code. The houses of faith had to close their doors; people began hearing from God through the Internet. Rev. O was invited to share her story through Zoom, and people listened and healed.

I never expected the Interruptions in my life or the importance of Disrupting the Silence about trauma and racial inequity for communities of color. Like everyone else, I am wrestling with the time when I had different dreams for my life.

Six months before I finished this book, my brothers' suspicion was confirmed. We discovered Duke had fathered a daughter while stationed in Denver, Colorado. Her name is Rev. Dr. Marcia Clinkscales.

After losing my son, suffering a brain aneurysm, and almost dying, God gave me a biological sister, and I do not stutter anymore.

Mother Mary

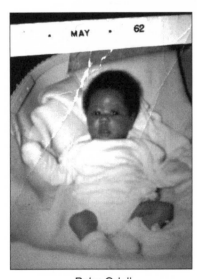

Baby Odell   Sarah, Nana and Me @1 year old

Nana, Odell and
Mother Mary

Momma Doe

I meet my brothers, Ben, Montez, their mother
Wilma and nephew Monty (Duke Benjamin
Montgomery III)

Charlene, Odell and Sarah

Angel, Robin, Cindy, Odell in High School

Odell, Robin and Angel partying in NY while at
Pratt

Alpha Phi Alpha
Fraternity, Inc.
(Darsweil) @ Howard
University Spring
Break

Robin, Angel, Odell
and Sarah—Howard
University Graduation

Cornell Dining Cross
Country Gourmet
dinner with staff

Wedding Day, Michael and Odell

Roger, Odell and JoAnn—
Wedding Day

Renewal of wedding vows—Pastor
McCorn, Odell, Michael and
Jonathan

Margarette and Arynce meet
Jackie and John

Nana and her siblings—Thompson Family

Uncle Lyle, Aunt Eleanor, Odell, Jody, Jonathan and Jackie

Arynce, Margarette and her husband Chris, Jonathan and Jackie. I was committed to make sure the siblings stayed connected

Jackie gets a tattoo in FAMU

Godfather Tony, James (business partner), Charlie and Odell

Damar, Marcel and
Jonathan

NY friends Justin,
Delfina with Jonathan

Jonathan, Odell and
Jackie, last family
photo at ConnCAT

Rev. Dr. Carl Dudley and Odell—Graduation Day from
Hartford Seminary Master's Program

Odell and
Dr. Edward
at Tai Chi
after brain
aneurysm

Soror Odell and Soror Dr. Joy
reconnect after 30 years

Rev. Odell is ordained at Mount Aery Baptist
Church by Rev. Dr. Bennett

Odell and KimBianca at
MGM Casino Grand Opening

Paris and Odell at Dallas Cowboys
stadium

Interruptions
Production Staff

Odell, Father Duke and sister
Rev. Dr. Marcia Montgomery
Clinkscales

Made in the USA
Middletown, DE
07 November 2021